AN ILLUSTRATED GUIDE TO THE
ANCIENT MONUMENTS
MAINTAINED BY THE DEPARTMENT OF THE ENVIRONMENT

ABBEYS
An Illustrated Guide to the Abbeys of England and Wales

R Gilyard-Beer OBE, MA, FSA

Formerly Assistant Chief Inspector of Ancient Monuments

London

Her Majesty's Stationery Office

ISBN 0 11 670776 3

Contents

Illustrations

Plans

(*pages* 59 *to* 88)

The Monks

Abbeys, priories, nunneries and friaries

"Abbey" is perhaps the most common of many words, each with its own shade of meaning, used to describe the monastic establishments that were a familiar feature of life in England and Wales for almost a thousand years. The terms of widest application are "convent" and "religious house," which simply mean a community of monks or nuns. A house of monks is usually called a "monastery," and one of nuns a "nunnery," and both monasteries and nunneries may have the title of "abbey" or "priory." The distinction here is one of status: an abbey is presided over by an abbot in the case of monks, or an abbess in the case of nuns, while a priory has no resident abbot and is presided over by a prior or prioress; a priory is usually an off-shoot from, and dependent upon, an abbey.

Houses of regular canons—that is to say, canons living under a monastic rule, as opposed to secular canons who normally serve cathedral churches—are also classified as abbeys and priories. In addition to all these, there are two other type of religious houses that have special names; houses of friars and houses of Carthusian monks, although often known as priories, are called "friaries" and "charterhouses" respectively.

This list of definitions, although useful for an accurate understanding of monastic remains, represents monasticism in its fullest development during the Middle Ages, when distinctions were made between various types of convent, and its specialised terms cannot be applied to early monasticism, the origins of which were very simple.

Hermits and monks

The predecessor of the monk was the hermit: the man who withdrew from the world and its temptations to devote himself in solitude to the service of God. It was from the grouping together of hermits that true monastic life emerged.

This grouping, whereby the hermit became the monk, following the same ideals but as a member of a community of men of like intention, can best be followed through its gradual development in the Near East where, by the second half of the fourth century AD, the customs of communal life and worship had been established by St Anthony, St Pachomius and St Basil. From its cradle in Egypt and the adjacent lands, early monasticism spread to Italy, to North Africa and to France; and it was with the foundation of such monasteries as Lérins and Marmoutier in the south and west of France that it found itself well placed to exercise an influence on Britain.

The invasions of the heathen Angles and Saxons in the fifth and sixth centuries, by penning Christianity into the western parts of Britain and by cutting its direct communications with the Continent on the south-east, gave a new lease of life to the western sea and land routes that had been in common use before the Roman Conquest, and it was along these routes that monasticism was directed in the first place to Galloway, Ireland and Wales, and later reached Northumbria from St Columba's foundation at Iona. The early monasticism of northern England therefore had a Celtic and Mediterranean complexion due to its descent through Ireland from the early monasteries of France. The northern monks, however, were not first in the field for, a few years before their arrival, monasticism had reached Kent from a different source.

The Benedictines

In 529 St Benedict of Subiaco had founded a monastery at Monte Cassino in Italy, and had compiled for its monks a set of regulations that became the basis of practically the whole of later monasticism in medieval Europe. The strength of the Benedictine Rule, as it came to be called, lay in the fact that the wisdom and moderation of its provisions could be universally applied, and its success was assured when, towards the end of the sixth century, it received the powerful support of Pope Gregory the Great.

Gregory himself was responsible for introducing the Benedictines into Britain, when he sent St Augustine, from the monastery of St Andrew in Rome, with a band of missionaries, to attempt the conversion of heathen England. With St Augustine's foundation of the monastery of St Peter and St Paul at Canterbury in 598 the Benedictines started a continuous history of almost a thousand years in this country.

The conversion of heathen England was therefore accomplished by two forces, advancing from opposite directions and each carrying with it a different form of monastic life. These differences of inspiration and observance made conflict inevitable, the crisis being marked by the introduction of the Benedictine Rule into the Celtic monastery of Ripon shortly after the middle of the seventh century, and the victory of the southern party by the Synod of Whitby in 664. But English monasticism was given a quiet life of little more than a century before it was almost entirely destroyed by the Danish invasions, and another century elapsed before conditions occurred that were favourable to its revival. Only Canterbury and the Celtic monasteries of Wales and the west maintained a continuous existence.

The revival came with a general reform of the English Church in the second half of the tenth century. The moving spirits of this reform, Archbishop Dunstan of Canterbury, Archbishop Oswald of York and Bishop Ethelwold of Winchester, had all been monks and were active in refounding old monasteries, in founding new ones, and in replacing congregations of secular priests by monks. St Dunstan and St Oswald both had practical experience of continental monasticism on which to base their work, and their wisdom in drawing up a single code of observance for all the monasteries in their charge gave the monastic life of the country a stability which encouraged a remarkable development of learning and of the arts.

The Cluniacs and black canons

Throughout the whole of its history there was a tendency for monasticism to fall away from its primitive zeal and austerity, giving rise to one attempt after another within the monastic body to restore observances to their early form. One such reform originated with the foundation of the abbey of Cluny in Burgundy at the beginning of the tenth century, and a succession of notable abbots ensured a prominent role for it during the Middle Ages. Starting simply as an attempt to restore the full observance of the Benedictine Rule, it developed features peculiar to itself during the tenth and eleventh centuries, two of the most characteristic being an emphasis on elaborate liturgy and ceremonial, and a centralised organisation in which monasteries founded by Cluny remained dependent priories under the control of the abbot of the mother-house. Its influence extended beyond these direct dependencies, and was felt in England during the tenth-century reform of the Church, for St Oswald had been a monk of Fleury, a French monastery reformed under Cluniac inspiration.

It was felt again after the Norman Conquest, for a similar inspiration had already been responsible for reforming the monasteries of Normandy, before William I's organisation of the English Church on Norman lines threw open a new field to its activities. During the latter part of the eleventh century, Norman ideas and Norman personnel changed the whole character of English monasticism, and set a pattern that lasted throughout the rest of the Middle Ages. Old monasteries, often under Norman abbots, were reorganised under the direction of two archbishops of Canterbury, Lanfranc and St Anselm, who had themselves been monks; new monasteries were founded by the King and his followers; and the monasteries of Normandy were enriched by grants of property and tithes and by the foundation of English and Welsh dependencies. One feature reminiscent of the Celtic Church was perpetuated in this Norman reorganisation, and became characteristic of medieval

England. This was the establishment of the seats of bishops in some of the more important monasteries, the monastic church being used as the cathedral, and the bishop standing in place of the abbot while the day-to-day business of governing the convent devolved on the prior. Nine of the medieval English sees were of this type, eight of them served by Benedictines, and the ninth by Augustinian Canons Regular.

Houses of Augustinian canons had begun to be founded in England from the end of the eleventh century. They derived from continental attempts to reform communities of priests serving large non-monastic churches. These attempts crystallised into an Order organised on monastic lines, and differing from the monks mainly in that all the members of its convents were priests, whereas until the fourteenth century it was unusual for every monk to enter the priesthood. They were popularly known as black canons from the colour of their habit, in the same way as the Benedictines and Cluniacs came to be known as black monks, and their foundations spread rapidly throughout England and Wales during the twelfth century, although with few exceptions their houses were of modest size and were governed by priors.

The reformed Orders

While Norman monasticism was being introduced into England and Wales, signs of dissatisfaction with the Cluniac influence that had played no small part in its development were already appearing on the Continent, where a reaction in favour of a more austere form of religious life was finding much support. The late eleventh and early twelfth centuries saw the creation of a series of new religious Orders which, no longer content to aim at restoring the Benedictine Rule in its purity, were prepared to go beyond its provisions in their search for greater austerity. Some were influenced by the ideals of the early hermits, and most sought to replace the Cluniac emphasis on liturgical duties by an emphasis on the importance of manual labour. Their weakness lay in their number and their similarity, and only one achieved popularity and strength in any way comparable to Cluny.

This was the Cistercian Order, which took its name from the abbey of Cîteaux in Burgundy, founded in 1098. The sites chosen for Cistercian houses were remote from towns, and the energy of their monks found an outlet in agricultural enterprise on a large scale. A special class of monks, the lay brethren, and a more highly organised type of grange or farm were used in the working of the estates and to preserve the seclusion of the quire-monks who,

Plate 1   WHITBY ABBEY; THE CHURCH FROM THE NORTH-WEST

from their unbleached habit, were known as white monks in contra-distinction to the black monks and canons. The Cistercian constitutions improved on the Cluniac idea of dependence on the mother-house by creating a system of mutual visitation and an annual meeting of all the abbots of the Order at Cîteaux, to maintain discipline and to ensure that legislation kept pace with contemporary needs. The Order spread rapidly on the Continent and in Britain. The first English foundation was made at Waverley in Surrey in 1128, but the main expansion was in the north of England and in Wales, where a comparative dearth of monasteries of the older Orders, coupled with great tracts of uncultivated land, gave scope for pioneering.

The other Orders which sprang from this monastic renaissance included those of Grandmont and Tiron, which established few houses in this country, while the Order of Savigny, although enjoying initial popularity, lacked outstanding leaders and was so similar to the Cistercians that it was merged with them before the middle of the twelfth century. The Order of Fontevrault is of importance in this country mainly for the influence of its constitution on the only monastic Order of purely English foundation—the Gilbertine Order.

The Gilbertine organisation, like that of Fontevrault, bore some resemblance to one feature of Celtic monasticism, in that many of the communities were double houses for men and women. The founder, St Gilbert of Sempringham, gave the Benedictine and Cistercian Rules to the nuns and lay sisters of his houses, while the men were canons following the Augustinian Rule and ministering to the spiritual needs of the nuns in place of the chaplains who normally served nunneries of other Orders.

During the latter part of the twelfth century a stricter Order of canons established a considerable number of houses in England, especially in the midlands and the north, and a single house in Wales. They were known as Premonstratensians from their first house at Prémontré in the Soissonnais, and as white canons from the colour of their habit, and their organisation showed strong Cistercian influence. Two Orders of lesser importance made use of the Rule of St Augustine; these were the Bonshommes and the Trinitarians, with only two and ten foundations respectively in this country.

Standing apart from all these in the extreme austerity of their lives, in the fervour with which they maintained their ideals throughout the Middle Ages and indeed up to the present day, and in the details of their organisation and buildings, were the Carthusian monks. They came closer than any of their contemporaries to the hermits from whose colonies monasticism had originally developed. Their Order took its name from a monastery in the valley of the Grande Chartreuse in Dauphiné, founded by St Bruno in 1084. Charterhouses were designed to provide a separate cell for each monk, in which he worked, prayed, ate and slept in a solitude that was complete except for attendance at certain communal meals and services. The austerity of the life kept down the number of recruits, and consequently the number of houses. One foundation was made in England in the latter part of the twelfth century, and another followed in the thirteenth, but the expansion of the Order did not come until between 1343 and 1414 when seven more houses were founded.

The friars

The popularity of the Carthusians in the later Middle Ages contrasted with the state of the other Orders at that time. During the twelfth century the number of monasteries in England and Wales had increased fourfold; during the thirteenth century the impetus slackened; after the middle of the fourteenth century practically no new houses of monks and canons were founded.

Early monasticism appealed to the medieval mind as a living example of successful organisation based on Christian principles. But as the centuries passed and the general level of civilisation rose, the monasteries lost their dominant position as repositories of learning, models of organised community life, leaders in architectural and artistic enterprise and sources of education. Nor did all the reformed Orders maintain the zeal that had inspired their foundation, so that in time it became increasingly difficult to differentiate between them and their older fellows. The price of this was paid in decreasing public sympathy and when, in the first half of the thirteenth century, the exponents of a radically different conception of religious life arrived in England, still more support was drawn away from the monks and canons.

The newcomers were the friars. First, the Dominicans or black friars, then the Franciscans or grey friars, and after them a number of similar Orders including the Augustinian friars and the Carmelites or white friars.

The aim of the monks had been to create a form of community life in which they could carry out their self-imposed discipline of worship and labour undisturbed, as far as possible, by contact with the outside world. The purpose of the friars was not to cloister themselves from the world, but to go out into it, seeking to influence the people by their preaching and by the example of their lives. At first they captured the popular imagination, but about a century after their arrival in England they suffered a partial eclipse in public favour and, like the monks, they could show few new foundations after the middle of the fourteenth century.

The alien priories

If few new monasteries were founded after the fourteenth century, nevertheless very few became extinct from natural causes, and the first serious reduction in their numbers proved to be a source of strength rather than weakness to the monastic body as a whole.

The position of " alien" religious houses in England and Wales had long been anomalous. They were direct dependencies of continental houses, generally owing their origin to benefactions made by William I's followers from newly acquired English and Welsh estates to the monasteries of their native lands. They varied in size and importance from fully developed priories where the regular life was practised in all its aspects, to simple farms where one or two monks from the mother-house resided to attend to the administration of its lands; yet they were alike in that, in time of war between England and France, they incurred the displeasure of the King, who was naturally unwilling to see revenue from English estates being dispatched across the Channel to monasteries in enemy territory. Frequent confiscation of their property was inevitable. Nor did their existence enhance the reputation of the monastic body in general for, in the case of very small dependencies, it was impossible for a handful of monks to live a full religious life, separated as they were by long distances from the discipline and inspiration of their mother-house, with their time heavily occupied by administrative duties, and their communications repeatedly cut by political disturbance.

Some of the larger alien priories put an end to this unsatisfactory state of affairs by breaking their continental connections and becoming "denizen" or naturalised. The position of the remainder was regularised after 1414 by their becoming dependencies of larger English houses, or by suppression and the transfer of their property to collegiate and educational foundations.

Daily life and organisation

Before considering the buildings in which the monks lived, something must be said of their life of constant prayer and work, to which the fabric of the monastery was no more than a background.

The "horarium" or timetable by which the daily life of the monk was regulated varied not only according to the seasons of the year, but also as between ordinary days and days of fasting. In addition

Plate 2   LLANTHONY PRIORY; THE CHURCH FROM THE NORTH-WEST

to this, the difference of emphasis placed by various Orders, and even by individual houses, on particular aspects of monastic life led to the compilation of sets of customs or "observances." The elaborate ceremonial of the Cluniacs, the early Cistercian insistence on simplicity and labour, and the Carthusian desire for solitary prayer, all led to modifications in the daily programme. There is only space here to give the framework of one such timetable as an example— the winter horarium devised by Archbishop Lanfranc for his Bene-dictine cathedral-monastery at Canterbury.

The monastic "day" at Canterbury began about 2.30am, when the monks were roused from sleep and came down from the dorter to take their places in quire. Psalms and prayers were followed by Nocturns, the first service, and this by Matins. If by the end of these services dawn had not yet broken, there was an interval of waiting before Prime, the next service. After Prime the monks sat and read in the cloister until about 8am, when it was time for them to return to the dorter, change their shoes, wash, and go back to the church for Terce and the Morrow Mass. After Mass the daily chapter was held, and then came a fairly long period of reading or work, lasting until about noon, when they returned to the church for Sext, High Mass and None. At the end of this, perhaps about 2pm, they went to the frater for the only substantial meal of the day, and then spent the afternoon in work or study until about 5pm. Vespers in church marked the end of the active day, and afterwards the monks changed into their night shoes, went to the frater for a drink, and then back to the church to listen to a short reading and for Compline, the last service. At the end of Compline, about 6.30 or 7pm, they retired to the dorter to sleep until the bell roused them for Nocturns and the beginning of another day.

Efficient organisation and a staff of monk officials with specialised duties were needed if a convent was to keep to such a timetable and at the same time attend to the provisioning of the house, the administration of its estates, and the many activities that ensured its continued existence.

The head or president of the convent, possessing absolute authority within the provisions of the Rule and within the precincts of his house, was the abbot. In early times, living, sleeping and eating with his monks, he was in a very true sense the father of the community. Later, however, the increasing demands of external business in the interests of his abbey tended to deprive him of these opportunities, and practical responsibility for the daily discipline of the convent sometimes devolved on his principal lieutenant and deputy, the prior, assisted by a sub-prior and, in large monasteries, by a "third prior."

The number of the remaining monk officials, known as obedientiaries, varied according to the size of the convent, and several are mentioned later in connection with the buildings where they performed their duties. Among the most important were the precentor, who arranged the services in church, the sacrist, who was responsible for the church furniture and fittings, and the cellarer who looked after the provisioning of the house.

The dissolution

At the beginning of the sixteenth century there were some eight hundred religious houses, large and small, in England and Wales. This number had remained more or less constant, but the total numbers of monks, nuns, canons and friars had fluctuated. After the middle of the fourteenth century their numbers were practically halved, and it was at this time that the Cistercian lay brethren virtually disappeared from the monastic scene. During the later Middle Ages there was a steady increase in recruitment, so that by the sixteenth century the monastic population was about three-quarters the size it had been at the time of its greatest expansion.

The destruction of the monasteries, and the abolition of medieval monastic life in this country, came through political action on the part of the King, and was carried out by means of Acts of Parliament. By an Act of 1536 the smaller religious houses of less than £200 annual value were dissolved, and their inmates given pensions or transferred to larger houses. The monastic body had therefore already been seriously depleted when a general visitation starting in 1538 procured the surrender of the remaining great houses.

By the end of 1540 the process of dissolution was complete. The majority of the monks, canons and nuns, who had conformed to the new Acts, were dispersed with pensions or appointed to benefices; the minority whose conscience had prompted them to open resistance had paid with their lives; and the buildings and estates had passed into the royal hands, later to be sold to laymen, except where they were used for the foundation of new bishoprics at Bristol, Chester, Gloucester, Oxford, Peterborough and, for a short time, Westminster.

The Buildings

Pre-Conquest monasteries

The little that is known about the arrangements of monasteries before the Norman Conquest comes partly from documentary and partly from archaeological evidence. The early houses founded under the influence of the Celtic Church, whether in Wales and the west during the Dark Ages, or in the north as a result of the mission of St Columba and his disciples, bear little resemblance to the plan that was later used throughout western Europe during the Middle Ages.

True to their eastern origin, the Celtic monasteries resembled groups of hermits' cells rather than communal establishments. The monks had individual cells, and there are comparatively few records or traces of buildings intended to serve the community as a whole, although there was a common dorter at Hackness, and the remains of what may have been a frater or dining hall have been excavated at Whitby, and a "scriptorium" or writing room at Tintagel. In addition to its principal church the late seventh-century monastery at Abingdon had an oratory to each of its monks' cells, and the whole collection of buildings was surrounded by a wall. Some such form of enclosure, designed partly to prevent the monks from being distracted by the sight of the outside world, was a constant feature. At Iona it was a bank; at Oundle a hedge.

The bleak and remote sites often chosen for these monasteries—Whitby on its cliff facing the North Sea; Tintagel on its rocky peninsula—were the northern equivalents of the deserts in which the eastern hermits had sought refuge. Excavations have shown something of the character of the buildings. At Tintagel (Figure 1, ii) five groups of dry-built stone huts have been found, belonging to a monastery probably established by St Juliot about the beginning of the sixth century. Roughly rectangular in plan, they cling precariously to the rocky ledges of the promontory, and are not grouped in any recognisable pattern. At Whitby (Figure 1, iii), an Anglian double monastery for men and women founded in the middle of the seventh century, similar rectangular stone cells have been found, but in this case they were free-standing and not grouped together. They were served by a complicated system of drainage and by a larger building which may have been a frater.

The Italian mission of St Augustine is represented by his monastery at Canterbury, which had three churches (Figure 1, i). Excavations beneath the later church of St Augustine's Abbey have brought to light the foundations of the church of St Peter and St Paul with its "porticus" or side chapels in which were buried King Ethelbert of Kent and the early archbishops of Canterbury. In line to the east of it were the similar but smaller churches of

Plate 3 *BUILDWAS ABBEY; THE CHURCH AND CLOISTER FROM THE NORTH-WEST*

St Mary and St Pancras. Multiple churches were characteristic of several early monasteries, such as Ripon and Hexham. The earliest Benedictine houses also show a more coherent arrangement of communal buildings than the Celtic ones, proved by excavation at Monkwearmouth and Jarrow.

After the tenth-century reforms of St Dunstan, at both Canterbury and Glastonbury, the small earlier churches were linked to form a single larger church, in emulation of the large monastic churches being built on the Continent. At Canterbury this was done in the eleventh century by the addition of a "rotunda" or round church, a plan derived from the Continent and also used in England at Bury St Edmunds. But the formal arrangement of monastic buildings round a cloister, known abroad from the early ninth century, does not seem to have been imitated. At Canterbury a courtyard existed north of the church but insufficient evidence has survived to show the exact arrangement of the buildings associated with it. The true claustral plan first introduced under Norman influence at Westminster about 1045 remained an exception and, even in the years following the Conquest, the Saxon community at Winchester did not adopt it in building the New Minster.

The medieval plan

That evidence for the appearance of pre-Conquest monasteries should be so rare is largely due to the radical changes made by the Normans. Not only were they responsible for a large number of new foundations, but the introduction of Norman abbots into monasteries of pre-Conquest foundation was almost invariably the signal for general rebuilding. Even allowing for the great amount of rebuilding done later in the Middle Ages, the plans and proportions of the majority of English monasteries are those given to them in Norman times.

The essential parts of this plan were the church, the buildings in which the monks lived, the buildings in which they cared for their sick and dispensed hospitality to their guests, and the buildings which served the day-to-day maintenance of the community and the exploitation of its estates.

The medieval arrangement of these parts was at once simple and practical (Figures 2 and 3). The church generally occupied the highest ground on the site and formed one side of a quadrangle known as the cloister, along the other three sides of which were ranged the buildings in which the monks lived. Such contacts as were necessary with the outer world took place in buildings grouped in an outer courtyard called the "curia," generally placed west of the cloister. The quarters of the sick, for the sake of peace and quiet,

lay on the opposite side of the cloister to the outer court. A precinct
wall entered through one or more gatehouses surrounded the whole.

The church

As the main purpose of a monk's life was the service of God, the
most important building of the monastery was its church in which,
unless he was an obedientiary with administrative duties to perform,
more than half his waking hours might be spent. Except in the
smallest monasteries, the plan of the church was in the form of a
cross, and it consisted of a presbytery, a quire, transepts usually with
chapels on their eastern side, and a nave.

The presbytery. Among the black monks, the plan of the presbytery
or eastern arm of the church generally conformed in Norman times
to one or other of two types that occur at an earlier date in Normandy itself. In the more ambitious plan, the east end was apsidal
and the aisles were carried round the apse as an ambulatory or
processional way from which three "bubble" chapels projected to
the north, south and east. The best surviving example is at Norwich,
where both side chapels remain intact although the eastern chapel
has been replaced by later work. Crypts reflecting the same plan can
be seen at St Augustine's, Canterbury (Figure 4, i) and Bury
St Edmunds, and foundations of this type of presbytery have been
excavated at Muchelney and Leominster. At Lewes, the provision
of five chapels instead of the normal three, in imitation of the
mother-house of Cluny, is typical of Cluniac elaboration.

   In the second type of plan, the main body of the presbytery and
each of its aisles ended in a separate apse, the latter often built
square externally, as formerly at Durham. St Albans (Figure 5, i) and
Binham before their later alterations were typical large and small
examples, and the Cluniacs used the plan in their early churches at
Castle Acre (Figure 5, iii) and Thetford. As the chapels on the
eastern sides of the transepts were usually apsidal in Norman
times, churches built to this second plan could present an imposing
array of apses to the east; at York, for instance, a line of seven
apses was graduated back on either side of the presbytery by the
expedient of making the inner transept chapels deeper than the
outer ones.

   The popularity of the apse did not last long in England and
Wales, and the more typical square east end, still associated with
apsidal aisles, is occasionally found alongside it. An early twelfth-
century example can be seen in the nuns' church at Romsey, and
the eastern arms of Dover and of the farmery chapel at Lewes had
this plan at about the same date. The abandonment of the apse in

favour of the square east end became general by the middle of the twelfth century, and lasted with few exceptions until the end of the Middle Ages.

Among the variety of plans that succeeded these apsidal east ends, three main types can be recognised. One had a square east end around which the aisles were returned, generally with a Lady Chapel projecting eastwards and roofed at a lower level than the main body of the church. The greater churches of the south and west favoured this arrangement, and monastic examples can be seen at Winchester and St Albans (Figure 5, ii).

But this elaborate type of presbytery was only suitable for great abbeys, and a second plan was found to be more fitting for churches of modest size. This had a square-ended presbytery flanked by short aisles, and it was used not only by the black monks but also by the canons regular, whose churches rarely equalled the dimensions of the older Benedictine abbeys. Castle Acre (Figure 5, iv) and Lanercost (Figure 13, i) are good examples of this plan, and in some cases—Titchfield and Alnwick, for instance—the aisles are so short that they may perhaps be regarded as deep transept chapels. Nor were aisles always thought necessary. The Benedictines dispensed with them at Lindisfarne, the Cluniacs at Monk Bretton, the Augustinians at Brinkburn and the Premonstratensians at Easby (Figure 8, iv) and other churches.

On the Continent, the successor of the apsidal east end was the "chevet," in which the main arcade was carried round as an apse, with an ambulatory and contiguous radiating chapels outside it. The Benedictines used this plan in its fully developed form at Westminster in the thirteenth century (Figure 4, iii) and later at Battle, Tewkesbury and Coventry, but it was not popular in England and Wales, and the square east end remained practically unchallenged among the monastic Orders.

It has already been seen that several of the Orders which first reached this country in the twelfth century had been founded at the height of a general movement in favour of austerity and simplicity, and some of them, including the Cistercians, the Carthusians, and the Grandmontines, had framed statutes to ensure that their buildings should be plain and humble. In the following century the case of the friars was similar, and it was natural that the early churches of these Orders should bear a family likeness, irrespective of their actual date, in that their plans were influenced by a common desire to have a building that should be as simple as was compatible with ritual needs.

The essential requirement was a rectangular, aisleless building, narrow in proportion to its length, and often with no structural

Plate 4   BYLAND ABBEY; THE WEST FRONT OF THE CHURCH

division between nave, quire and presbytery. Hulne has a good Carmelite church (Figure 6, ii), Lincoln a Franciscan one (Figure 6, iii), and Brecon a Dominican one (Figure 6, iv), all of simplest plan. The best surviving Carthusian examples are the lay brothers' church at Witham, and the church of Mount Grace to which the transeptal chapels and tower are later additions. The early plan of the London Charterhouse was also similar (Figure 6, v). Two of the three Grandmontine houses in England, while keeping the essential simplicity of this plan, had a curious apsidal east end of greater width than the nave (Figure 6, i, and Figure 14, ii), a peculiarity inherited from the continental houses of their Order.

Comparatively few of the earliest church plans of the larger monasteries of the austere Orders are known, because later rebuilding has destroyed all traces of them above ground. They differed from the plain rectangles described above only in their possession of transepts. The first churches of the Cistercians were sometimes of wood, but the plans of two stone ones have been recovered by excavation at Waverley (Figure 14, i), the first house of the Order in England, and at Tintern (Figure 6, vii). They show a strong resemblance to the early church of the Augustinians at Haughmond (Figure 6, vi), also known from excavation, and to such simple Premonstratensian churches as Torre (Figure 6, viii). Simplicity could hardly be carried further in a church of cross-plan. Each consists of an aisleless nave, short transepts with rectangular chapels to the east, and a short, aisleless, square-ended presbytery. This characteristic plan satisfied at one and the same time the early Cistercian mistrust of architectural elaboration and the English preference for a square-ended church.

The retention of this modest type of presbytery was a special feature of Cistercian planning during the twelfth century, even after the rapid increase in the popularity and numbers of the Order had led to an equally marked increase in the scale of its churches. Normally no more than two bays in length, it is the distinguishing feature of the classical Cistercian plan associated by continental scholars with the name of St Bernard of Clairvaux, and represented in England and Wales by such examples as Kirkstall and Valle Crucis (Figure 7, i).

Before the century was out, however, the gradual relaxation of early Cistercian severity in architecture, coupled with a pressing need for more altars as the custom grew for more monks to enter the priesthood, caused the plan to be not so much abandoned as logically developed. At Dore an aisled presbytery of three bays was built, with an eastern aisle giving access to a row of five chapels beyond it. At Byland (Figure 7, ii), also of three bays, the eastern aisle itself was divided into chapels, and access to it was from the eastern bay of the presbytery, the high altar being placed one bay to the west. The end of the process can be seen at Jervaulx (Figure 7, iii) where both ambulatory and chapels were brought under the high roof of the church by siting the altar two bays from the east end. The presbytery of Jervaulx is of four aisled bays, as are those of Netley and Tintern, but a natural extension of this form led to the great eastern arms that were the pride of northern abbeys of practically all the Orders: Augustinian Thornton (Figure 8, ii), of six bays, Cistercian Rievaulx (Figure 7, iv) and Benedictine Whitby of seven, Augustinian Carlisle and Kirkham of eight, and Benedictine York (Figure 8, i) of nine. Fountains (Figure 10, ii) went even further, and to an aisled presbytery of five bays added an eastern transept like a great Tau cross on plan, a design so spectacular that it was copied by Durham (Figure 9, i).

A less ambitious form of extension was sometimes made simply by lengthening the original aisleless presbytery, as at Strata Florida (Fig. 8, v–vi). This was not peculiar to the Cistercians, and the Premonstratensians, who were influenced by Cistercian church design, were fond of it as an economical solution. Long and narrow presbyteries with a characteristically "lean and hungry look" are common to several of their churches, such as Easby (Figure 8, iii–iv).

Four Cistercian churches were among the very few in England that showed the influence of the chevet. The French Cistercians adopted it as early as the third quarter of the twelfth century, building presbyteries ending in an apse with encircling ambulatory and a crown of radiating chapels, but in many of their churches they modified it to suit their reputation for severity by enclosing the chapels with a continuous wall and not allowing them to project individually. In England this form was used early in the thirteenth century at Beaulieu, while later at Beaulieu's daughter-house of Hailes and at Vale Royal it was allowed to develop into the true chevet with projecting polygonal chapels. The plan used at Hailes also appeared at Croxden (Figure 7, v), probably through direct continental influence.

The presbytery contained the high altar, often standing clear of the east wall of the church and backed by a stone reredos as at Winchester and Durham. It had its attendant lockers, a piscina for rinsing the sacred vessels, and sedilia or seats for the officiating priests, many examples of which have survived.

The quire lay west of the presbytery, usually occupying the crossing and the eastern bays of the nave, an arrangement still to be seen at

Westminster and Gloucester. It was open to the presbytery on the east, but separated from the aisles, transepts and nave by screens. Sometimes, as at Ely and York, it had its own altar west of the high altar. Against the screens dividing the quire from the aisles and transepts were placed the stalls of the monks, those of the abbot and prior being on the south and north sides respectively of the doorway through the western screen. The development of English stall design is nowhere better represented than in monastic churches, from the early examples at Winchester, through the later fourteenth century at Gloucester and Chester, and the fifteenth century at Whalley and Carlisle, to the fragments of early sixteenth-century work from Bridlington and Jervaulx. When the stalls themselves have gone, the L-shaped foundations on which they stood can sometimes be recognised, equipped at Fountains with earthenware jars let into the masonry to improve the acoustics. Between the lines of stalls stood the lectern, the position of which can be seen at Basingwerk and Titchfield from the socketed stone that held its shaft. Lecterns have survived at Norwich and Peterborough, and that of Newstead has found its way into Southwell Minster.

The screen closing the western end of the quire was known as the "pulpitum." It had a doorway in the centre, with an altar on each side against its western face, and a loft above, on which the organs were sometimes placed. To give room for these arrangements the screen was often double and occupied a full bay of the nave, but the mutilation of the ritual arrangements of churches at the Reformation has left few examples intact. Norwich has a stone pulpitum restored in the nineteenth century, and Hexham a particularly fine wooden one.

West again of the pulpitum and its altars was the rood screen, with an altar against its western face, a doorway on either side, and the great Rood or crucifix with its attendant figures above. Rood screens remain at St Albans and Tynemouth, and their foundations or the holes for the rood beam at many other abbeys. A few of the greater churches with very long eastern arms did not permit the quire to encroach on the structural nave. At the cathedral-monasteries of Canterbury and Durham (Figure 9, i), for instance, the rood screen was placed beneath the western arch of the crossing and the pulpitum beneath the eastern arch, the quire thus being confined to the eastern arm, and a similar arrangement was adopted at Rievaulx (Figure 7, iv) and Castle Acre (Figure 5, iv) when they lengthened their structural presbyteries.

Transepts generally had chapels opening from their eastern sides. At first these were apsidal, like those still to be seen at Romsey and

Plate 5 *LANERCOST PRIORY; THE CROSSING*

Tewkesbury, but they soon gave way to a simple eastern aisle with a chapel in each bay, separated at first by solid walls and later by screens.

The transept nearest the cloister housed the night stairs leading up to the adjoining dorter and giving the monks direct access to the church for the night offices. These stairs have rarely survived, but a perfect example remains at Hexham, and traces of them can often be recognised against the west wall of the transept, as at Neath where the moulded stone handrail remains. When space was limited, the stairs were sometimes contrived in the thickness of the west wall, as at Lacock (Figure 13, ii) and Haverfordwest, or took the form of a newel as at Lindisfarne and Ewenny. Cluniac houses like Castle Acre and Thetford (Figure 12), and the Augustinian house of Llanthony Prima dispensed with them altogether and had no direct communication between dorter and church.

In Cistercian houses, the transept on the side of the church away from the cloister usually had a doorway leading to the cemetery outside.

The nave in the greater churches of both black and white monks was often of great length. Seven bays as at Blyth and Buildwas, or eight as at Durham (Figure 9, i) and Roche (Figure 15) were common. Binham and Rievaulx were of nine bays, St Albans and Furness of ten, Peterborough and Fountains (Figure 10) of eleven, Winchester and Byland of twelve, and Norwich even extended to fourteen bays.

In the churches of the black monks and canons the nave was open to layfolk. Not infrequently it formed the parish church as at Wymondham and Brecon, and at Tynemouth (Figure 3) the parish priest had a house adjoining its north aisle. When the nave was parochial it was usually left standing at the dissolution and has served its purpose ever since, Binham and Bridlington being examples. At Crowland and Leominster one aisle alone served the parish, while at Sherborne the parish church abutted on the west end of the nave and at St Albans it lay outside the north aisle. Nor were the nave and its aisles the only parts of monastic churches used by the parish; at Chester the parishioners established squatters' rights in the south transept despite the fact that the abbot had built a new church for them. Cistercian nuns' churches in Germany often had the ritual quire at the west end of the nave, and an echo of this is found at Benedictine Marrick and Cistercian Nunkeeling where the nuns used the nave as their church and gave the eastern arm over to the parish.

The white monks used the nave as the church of their lay brethren

(Figure 10, i). Its aisles were shut off by solid stone screens, considerable remains of which can be seen at Tintern. At Strata Florida these screens are so much a part of the structure that the bases of the nave piers are set on top of them. Against the screens were placed the stalls of the lay brethren, the aisles serving only as passageways.

The churches of such small religious houses as Portchester dispensed with nave aisles altogether, and this was also the case with many of the nuns' churches, as in the thirteenth-century example at Nun Monkton; but the practice was not peculiar to small churches, and it occurs in quite large churches of the Orders of canons. The Augustinians of Kirkham and the Premonstratensians of Titchfield kept their aisleless naves until the dissolution, but in other cases a single aisle was provided on the side opposite the cloister, as at Bolton and Lanercost (Figure 13, i) where it did not necessitate an expensive replanning of the monastic buildings. Even at the rich Augustinian abbey of Thornton, where a complete rebuilding of the church and claustral buildings was undertaken shortly after the middle of the thirteenth century, and where the practical consideration of encroaching on an earlier cloister was unimportant, the new nave was designed with a north aisle only, and it was not until three bays had been built that the plan was revised and a south aisle was added.

In the houses of the black monks and canons, access from the cloister to the church was by means of two doorways set in the aisle wall against which the cloister abutted, and opposite its east and west alleys. When, on Sundays, the community in procession visited the altars in the church and made a ceremonial round of the claustral buildings, they left the church by the easternmost of these doorways and returned by the western one.

The Cistercians, whose Sunday procession followed a slightly different route to include in its course the lay brethren's rooms in the western range, sometimes had no doorway opposite the western alley, as at Jervaulx and Croxden, and returned to the church through the doorway at the west end of the nave or through a doorway in the western range itself. In the canons' and other small churches that had no nave aisle on the side of the cloister, there are often two eastern cloister doorways, one in the nave wall and the other leading eastwards into the transept, so that the presbytery could be reached without passing the nave altar or going through the quire. This arrangement can be seen at Lanercost (Fig. 13, i) and Ewenny, and a curious passage contrived in the thickness of the nave wall on the side away from the cloister at Kirkham served a similar purpose. In fully aisled churches, the aisle next to the cloister served as a passageway communicating through the transept with the presbytery. A stoup for holy water was provided outside (Lanercost) or inside (Rievaulx) the eastern cloister doorway.

The Sunday procession has also occasionally left traces of itself at the west end of the church and within the nave. The Cistercians, whose procession did not use the western cloister doorway, often had a small porch outside the west end of their churches. In early examples like Rievaulx and Fountains (Figure 10, 1) it was a lean-to covering the whole width of the church, with a dwarf wall supporting an open arcade on the west, but later churches like Tintern and Neath had a small but comparatively elaborate porch covering the west doorway only. These porches came to be known as "Galilees," because the abbot leading his monks in procession into the church was regarded as symbolising Christ going before His disciples into Galilee.

Within the nave, the procession made its final station at the nave altar, before which the abbot stood with his monks in two files behind him to north and south. The exact place where each monk was to stand was sometimes indicated on the nave pavement; at Fountains (Figure 10, ii) limestone slabs were let into the tiled pavement, and at Easby and Shap, where the nave was flagged in stone, the places are marked by incised circles.

The design of monastic churches was affected not only by changing architectural fashions, but also by other factors.

The Lady Chapel—One of these was the importance attached to the veneration of the Blessed Virgin, and the provision of large Lady Chapels. Where possible, the Lady Chapel took the form of an extension to the east end of the church, as at Thornton (Figure 8, ii) and Canterbury (Figure 4, ii). These chapels have rarely survived the destructive zeal of the Reformation, even in such abbey churches as Sherborne and Pershore that continued in use after the dissolution. Another favourite site for the Lady Chapel was parallel to the eastern arm of the church on the side away from the cloister; sometimes, as at Thetford (Fig. 12) and Lacock (Figure 13, ii) an integral part of the fabric, and sometimes, as in the magnificent fourteenth-century example at Ely, a detached building connected to the church by a passage.

Shrines—Several monasteries possessed relics of saints, the most celebrated instances in England being the relics of St Thomas à Becket and St Cuthbert in the cathedral-monasteries of Canterbury and Durham, and those of St Edward the Confessor at Westminster. The shrines enclosing these relics were usually given a place of

Plate 6   CASTLE ACRE PRIORY; AERIAL VIEW FROM THE NORTH-WEST

honour between the reredos of the high altar and the entrance to the Lady Chapel. The arrangement can be seen at Chester (Figure 11), where the shrine of St Werburgh has been restored to its old position, and at St Albans (Figure 5, ii) where the reliquary cupboards and a watching loft for the monks appointed to guard the shrine of St Alban have survived.

Chantries—The appearance of monastic churches was also much altered by the foundation of chantries, requiring prayers to be said for the souls of individual benefactors. When the benefactor himself was buried in the church, the opportunity of making his chantry an architectural feature was often embraced, and his tomb and chantry altar might be placed between the piers of the main arcade and enclosed by a wooden or stone open-work screen (Figure 9, i). Few of the greater abbey churches are without examples, and there are particularly fine series at Winchester and Christchurch. Important chantry chapels were also built as additions to the main fabric of the church. At Tynemouth, where the Lady Chapel lay north of the church, the Percy chantry took the form of a small chapel projecting from the east end of the presbytery; at St Augustine's, Canterbury (Figure 4, ii), and at Thetford (Figure 12) single small chapels were built outside the aisles of the nave. The gradual disappearance of the lay brethren in Cistercian monasteries during the later Middle Ages also led to the demolition of the screens dividing the nave from its aisles, and often to the foundation of small chapels in the bays of the aisles themselves, six of which remain at Rievaulx, Fountains (Figure 10, ii), and Byland.

Friars' churches—The later development of the friars' churches continued to show the influence of their constitutions. The popularity of the Cistercians in the twelfth and thirteenth centuries brought with it a host of benefactions that enabled them to enlarge the eastern arms of their churches in accordance with the architectural fashions of the times, so that there is little to choose in plan and elevational design between Cistercian Rievaulx and Benedictine Whitby, or in ritual arrangement between Fountains (Figure 10, ii) and Durham (Figure 9, i). The friars, on the other hand, while building larger churches, kept in mind the special duty of preaching that distinguished them from the monks and canons. The naves of their churches became preaching vessels with wide aisles and broad arcades, whilst their quires, except in the great London friaries, remained aisleless although they increased in length (Figures 19 and 20). The division between nave and quire in a friars' church was marked by two cross-walls between which a passage or "walking place" generally communicated with the domestic buildings, and when a steeple was added to the church it was placed on the line of these walls within the width of the church, and was often octagonal as at Lynn, Coventry and Atherstone.

Towers add distinction to the external appearance of most of the great abbey churches. Norman churches usually had a tower over the crossing, varying according to the size of the church from the small example at Portchester to the massive structures at St Albans and Tewkesbury. When funds permitted, the central tower was balanced by a pair of towers at the west end of the nave, as at Durham, or by a single western tower sometimes associated with a western transept as at Ely.

The Cistercian Rule forbade the building of large towers, and the typical early Cistercian tower, to be seen at Buildwas, consisted of little more than a wall over each arch of the crossing, high enough for the roofs of the church to butt against it. In later years the temptation to indulge in architectural display proved too strong, and some of the richer Cistercian abbeys started to build towers of considerable height. Kirkstall succeeded in heightening its old central tower, but in other cases this expedient proved disastrous because the crossing piers had not been intended to bear so great a weight. Buttresses erected against the crossing piers at Furness and Fountains show that attempts to raise their central towers had led to structural failure, and although a fine tower was eventually built at each of these abbeys it had to be placed at the west end of the nave at Furness and at the end of the north transept at Fountains.

The cloister

The position of the cloister in relation to the church was determined by the lie of the ground, and especially by the direction in which drainage to a river could most easily be achieved. If this consideration permitted, it was generally placed on the south side of the nave, so that it would catch the sun and not lie within the shade of the high roofs of the church. But northern cloisters are not uncommon, dictated by the position of the river as at Tintern and Buildwas. At Canterbury cathedral-monastery and Chester, where the site was in the north-eastern angle of a walled city, it may also have been felt that by placing the cloister on the side of the church furthest from the streets more quiet and seclusion could be obtained. Cloisters placed against the eastern arm of the church instead of against the nave are very rare, but there were examples at Rochester and Penmon.

Each side of the cloister had a covered alley, usually of one storey,

with a lean-to roof against the walls of the buildings. In the twelfth
and early thirteenth centuries the alley wall had an open arcade
standing on a dwarf wall; reconstructed portions of cloisters of this
type can be seen at Rievaulx and Newminster. The capitals of the
twin columns usually supporting the arcade provided the medieval
carver with an opportunity to show his virtuosity. Elaborate
examples have come from Reading, Bermondsey and Norwich. The
Cistercians, with their early dislike of elaboration, preferred conventional leaf-forms for the decoration of their cloister capitals, and
there are superb examples of this type at Byland.

These early cloisters with their open arcades must have been cold
and cheerless in winter, and attempts to make them more comfort-
able can sometimes be recognised, as at York where the capitals of
the arcade were chased to take wooden frames for temporary
glazing. With the invention of tracery, the arcades were replaced by
windows, at first open as at Westminster, but later glazed. Similarly,
early timber cloister roofs were replaced by stone vaulting.

The cloister alleys served other purposes besides acting as galleries
of communication between the building against which they were set.
The alley next to the church was a recognised place for the monks to
spend the periods allotted to them for reading and study, and here
are often found the stone benches on which they sat against the
church wall. Many cloisters had the more elaborate arrangement of
a series of cubicles set against the windows of the alley to form
separate studies known as carrells. These were normally of wainscot
and have therefore vanished, but a reconstructed set of stone ones
can be seen at Chester (Figure 11), and the famous cloister of
Gloucester—which is as fine an example as any of the late medieval
type with traceried windows and stone vaulting—has kept its
complete series of twenty.

Britain is fortunate in possessing a few examples of a rare Cistercian feature associated with these periods of study, and especially
with the Collation or reading before Compline. This is the abbot's
seat against the church wall, midway along the cloister alley. The
arched recess for his chair remains at Cleeve and Tintern, and the
position of the Collation lectern can also be traced at Strata Florida
and Tintern where it occupied a small bay projecting into the garth
of the cloister.

The books for use in the cloister were kept close at hand in a
shelved cupboard in the transept wall that overlapped the eastern
alley. At Durham the western alley had its own book cupboard to
serve the novices' school which was held there.

Most surviving cloisters are of one storey, but it was not uncommon for them to have an upper floor in the later Middle Ages, as at

Plate 7   RIEVAULX ABBEY: AERIAL VIEW FROM THE SOUTH-EAST

Muchelney. At Evesham, this upper floor was divided into private studies, and at St Albans it formed the library; but in some small monasteries and in the houses of friars the impression of a two-storeyed cloister is given by what is, in fact, a more economical method of planning, the cloister alleys being mere passages within the main walls of the buildings, and the upper rooms projecting over them and so gaining more floor-space (Figures 19 and 20). This expedient was adopted by the Gilbertines at Watton (Figure 18) and by several nunneries of modest size such as the Benedictine houses of Thicket and Wilberfoss (Figure 30) and the Cistercian houses of Handale and Kirklees. A surviving example can be seen at the Carmelite friary in Coventry.

The garth or space enclosed by the four alleys of the cloister was usually kept under grass, but there are instances of its being put to a more practical use, as at York where it served as a herb garden. Carthusian custom used part of it as a cemetery.

The dorter range

The eastern range of buildings surrounding the cloister was of two storeys, the whole of the first floor forming the *dorter* or dormitory of the monks, with a doorway to the night stairs in the adjacent transept. Comparatively few dorters are still roofed and floored, although there are good Benedictine examples at Westminster and Durham. None has kept the normal late medieval arrangement whereby the interior was divided by wainscot partitions into two rows of cubicles for the beds, with a passage down the middle.

There was always direct communication between the dorter and the *reredorter* or latrine block of the monastery, the position of which was dictated by the course of the main drain and therefore by the direction from which running water could be drawn. Sometimes, as at Lewes and Castle Acre, the reredorter was a building placed at the end of the dorter furthest from the church, and overlapping it to east and west. More commonly it projected eastwards from the dorter, about half-way down its length at Byland and Jervaulx or—a favourite position, adopted at Norwich, Finchale (Figure 29, ii) and many other houses—at its south-east angle. At Furness and Neath, where the drainage ran from north to south along the east side of the monastery, the reredorter was placed parallel to the east side of the dorter and was connected to it by a bridge.

The arrangement of the reredorter was simple. On the ground floor was the main drain, often notable for its fine masonry even in a fairly small house like Monk Bretton, and the origin of many a legend about secret passages. Above it, on the first floor, the seats were arranged in rows, either back to back or along one wall. An adequate supply of water for flushing the drains was not only an important factor in the selection of a site for a monastery, but also often influenced the planning of the buildings. Where the dorter occupied an unusual position, as at Worcester and Easby where it was in the western range, it was probably because drainage problems had led to the placing of the reredorter on that side of the cloister. No better example of this influence of drainage on monastic planning can be seen than Kirkham, where the main drain forms a quadrant on the south-east side of the claustral buildings, and the reredorter, prior's lodging, kitchens and farmery follow its course in a crescent of buildings more than 100yd long.

The ground floor of the dorter range was divided into several rooms, each with its doorway to the cloister. Next to the transept there was often a *slype* or passage leading through the range to the cemetery east of the church, as at Gloucester or Worcester, and sometimes also serving as the private or *inner parlour* where necessary conversation was allowed and where, at York, the obedientiaries met to discuss business later to be transacted in chapter.

The place of the slype was sometimes taken by a narrow room serving a variety of purposes: at Thornton partly as a parlour and partly as a strongroom or treasury with a complicated entrance from first-floor level, at Titchfield as a library with book presses against three of its walls, and at Thetford (Figure 12) and Easby as a *sacristy* with a doorway into the transept. The sacred vessels for use in the church were kept in the sacristy in the charge of the sacrist, an obedientiary who had in his care all the fittings and ornaments of the church and was also responsible for routine repairs to its fabric. Sacristies were always placed close to the church, but did not always form part of the buildings round the cloister. At the Cluniac houses of Castle Acre and Thetford (Figure 12) there were sacristies adjoining the transept opposite the cloister, each provided with a small oven for making the sacrificial wafers for the Mass. Several of the great northern monastic churches had sacristies against the south aisles of their long presbyteries; foundations of these remain at Whitby and York (Figure 8, i), and the best surviving example is the fine two-storeyed sacristy in this position at Selby.

The chapter house was the next room, second only to the church in importance. It adjoined the transept at Chester (Figure 11), Castle Acre, and other houses where no slype or sacristy occupied this position.

The convent assembled here each day after the Morrow Mass, the meeting beginning with a reading from the Martyrology, followed by collects and then by a chapter of the Rule, from which the room took its name. The obituaries for the day, and the lists of monks with special duties for the week were read, faults were confessed and punishment decreed. The temporal business of the house was also transacted here, and the room had many other uses connected with the corporate life of the convent. Here, in monasteries not exempt from episcopal visitation, the bishop usually held his periodical inquiries into the state of the convent.

The early chapter houses of the black monks often had an apse at the east end, as at Castle Acre (Figure 23, i) and Reading. Even when they were square-ended and later in date, as at Chester and York (Figure 23, iv), they projected eastwards from the range, and only houses of the modest size of Finchale (Figure 29, ii) and Monk Bretton (Figure 23, iii) kept them within the main walls of the range. Their importance in the life of the convent made them the subject of architectural elaboration, expressed at Much Wenlock and Bristol by rows of internal arcading, and almost everywhere by the presence of a window on each side of the doorway into the cloister.

Their height, especially when vaulted in stone, was generally greater than that of the other ground-floor rooms of the range, and various expedients were adopted to prevent the chapter house from cutting the dorter off from the transept. At Rochester and Bindon, the westernmost bay of the chapter house was vaulted at a lower level than the rest, to leave room for a passage above connecting the dorter and the night stairs, and in other cases, of which Chester is a good example, the whole of the space within the main walls of the range was treated as a vestibule with a low vault, and the chapter house proper was sited entirely to the east of the range.

This was especially necessary when the peculiarly English form of of a polygonal chapter house was adopted, for it was impossible to reconcile such a shape within the straight lines of the range. This can well be seen in the earliest known example of the type at Worcester, where no vestibule was built. Polygonal chapter houses with vestibules were built during the thirteenth and fourteenth centuries at houses of most of the major Orders; Benedictine Westminster (Figure 23, vii), Cluniac Pontefract, Augustinian Thornton, and Premonstratensian Cockersand can all show examples. At such a small priory as Bolton (Figure 23, vi) the vestibule could also be made to do duty as an inner parlour.

The Cistercians, with their customary restraint, preferred a rectangular chapter house divided by columns, almost invariably three bays wide but varying in length from three bays at Byland to

Plate 8   VALLE CRUCIS ABBEY; THE SOUTH TRANSEPT AND DORTER RANGE

six at Fountains (Figure 23, v). Dore, Margam and Whalley show that they did not always succeed in resisting the temptations of the attractive polygonal plan, but their most remarkable lapse from austerity is to be seen in the spacious twelfth-century chapter house at Rievaulx (Figure 23, ii) provided with not only an apse but an ambulatory as well.

The Cistercians also sometimes used the west end of the chapter house as a library. At Fountains and Furness the bays flanking the western entrance were partitioned off in stone for this purpose, and a single book closet is found in this position at the smaller houses of Calder and Valle Crucis.

Around the walls of the chapter house were the benches on which the convent sat during the meetings, the president's place being at the east end, sometimes marked architecturally as at Finchale and Canterbury, and sometimes by a break in the benching to accommodate his chair as at Fountains. In front of him stood the lectern, the socket of which remains at Byland and Waverley, and at his feet were the graves of his predecessors, for this was the recognised place of burial for the heads of convents until the fourteenth century.

The planning of the rest of the ground floor of the dorter range was not standardised. It had to accommodate the day stairs by which the monks reached the dorter during hours of daylight, the warming house, and, in those monasteries where there was no parlour or slype next to the transept, an inner parlour and a passage to the farmery. Parlour and slype were usually side by side, and the position of the latter was influenced by that of the farmery. At Westminster and Castle Acre, for instance, the slype was placed well to the south so that it should be opposite the farmery. The parlour, as at Thetford (Figure 12), might simply take the form of a space partitioned off from that part of the dorter undercroft projecting beyond the cloister.

The usual position of the *day stairs* was next to the chapter house on the side away from the church, again as at Thetford, but other positions were used when the cloister was small or the planning of the range had to be condensed. At Chester (Figure 11) the day stairs ascend in a thickening of the west wall of the range at the end of the cloister furthest from the church, and at Bolton they were in the east end of the frater range.

The last room in the range was the undercroft below the extension of the dorter beyond the cloister. The use to which it was put varied and cannot always be determined. At Bury St Edmunds the chamberlain had his quarters there; he was the obedientiary responsible for providing the convent with clothing and bedding.

Occasionally it was used by the novices, whose chapel lay on its eastern side at Peterborough. Some houses of black monks and canons, Thetford and Shap for example, used it as the *warming house* of the monastery, where a fire was kept burning during the winter months. The position of the warming house was to some extent influenced by that of the dorter, and in the rare instances where the latter is not in the east range, the warming house is to be found with it, as at Easby.

The frater range

The principal room in the range opposite the church was the *frater* (refectory) or dining hall of the monks. It generally occupied almost the whole of the range, and might be on the ground floor as at Chester, or raised above an undercroft as at Durham. In many houses there was a passage through the range to the east of the frater, giving access to the dorter undercroft and sometimes, as at Westminster, to the passage leading through that undercroft to the farmery. At Haughmond, Easby, and other houses where the outer court lay south instead of west of the cloister, this passage served as the outer parlour and entry to the cloister.

The internal arrangements of the frater were not unlike those of any medieval great hall. The entrance from the cloister was near the west end, and within the frater the tables were set parallel to the side walls, with the high table at the east end, where the officers of the house took their meals. On the wall behind the high table there was often a reredos; at Cleeve it was a painted Crucifixion, at Fountains a crucifix, and at Worcester and York a representation of Our Lord in Majesty.

Close to the high table there was a pulpit from which one of the brethren read aloud during the meals; it was reached by a stairway in a thickening of the south wall, and good examples have survived at Chester (Figure 11) and Shrewsbury. The pulpit stairs at Fountains have a small cupboard for the books used during the reading, and other small recesses and cupboards found in fraters, as at Haughmond and Hailes, were for spoons and table linen.

In the cloister near the frater doorway was the *lavatory* at which the brethren washed their hands at meal times and combed their beards in the mornings. It was usually a long trough in an arcaded recess in the frater wall, as at Rievaulx and Fountains, but at some houses like Haughmond and Kirkham it was in the west alley, and at Gloucester it was in the alley wall beneath the cloister windows. England had a few examples, at Much Wenlock, Exeter, Canterbury and elsewhere, of a type of lavatory that was more common on the Continent—an independent circular or polygonal pavilion in the cloister garth, with a central basin fed by a pipe or a series of taps. Towels were kept in a wall cupboard close by, as at Gloucester and Fountains.

The frater and its lavatory were in the charge of an obedientiary known as the refectorer, whose duty it was to provide table linen and lights, and to draw provisions from the cellarer.

The kitchen was usually a free-standing building on the side of the frater away from the cloister. It was generally rectangular, as at Castle Acre and Easby, but occasionally polygonal as at Durham and St Augustine's, Canterbury, or a square with fireplaces set diagonally in the four corners, as in the very complete abbot's kitchen at Glastonbury.

In some of the smaller houses economy in planning led to the kitchen being placed at the end of the west range nearest the frater. This was its position at Exeter, and in the later Middle Ages a few of the larger houses re-sited their kitchens in this way. Thetford (Figure 12), which in the twelfth century had a rectangular detached kitchen, converted the southern part of the cellarer's range to this use within fifty years of the dissolution, and its hand-mill, well and an impressive battery of ovens can still be seen.

Buttery and *pantry*—These were normally associated with the kitchen, and food was passed into the frater through a service hatch in one of the walls near its west end. Service hatches remain at Mattersey, Monk Bretton, and many other houses, and a pair of them giving on to a service lobby or large screens passage can be seen at Muchelney.

The cellarer's range

The main feature of the western range of claustral buildings was the *cellar* or great storehouse of the monastery, a ground-floor room or basement usually vaulted from a central row of columns, as at Chester (Figure 11) and Norton. It was in the charge of the cellarer, the most important of the obedientiaries not connected with the service of the church, who took care of the bulk provisioning of the convent. There was a practical reason for placing the cellar on this side of the cloister, for the outer court through which provisions reached the monastery usually lay to the west and the cellar therefore had direct access to it.

The only other room that was almost invariably placed on the ground floor of the range was the outer or *public parlour*, which formed an entrance from the outer court to the cloister, where conversation between the monks and layfolk could take place.

Plate 9   BRADFORD-ON-AVON; THE GREAT BARN WHICH SERVED SHAFTESBURY ABBEY (page 47)

Often it was no more than a passage through the range, but in some northern monasteries like Selby and Bridlington it was a large room projecting westwards. Its normal position was next to the nave of the church, and sometimes, as at York, there was also a second and more private entry through the range more or less opposite the west end of the south alley of the cloister.

The first floor of the range often housed the head of the convent or the guests, and might therefore be divided into several rooms, which will be dealt with later. When these rooms have vanished, the vaulting of the cellar sometimes betrays their arrangement—for example, at Norton and Bradenstoke, where it can be inferred that the first floor had a chapel, a hall and chamber, occupying one, four and three bays respectively of its total length. At Tynemouth the common hall for the servants of the monastery was here, and at such houses as Durham and Easby practical difficulties led to the dorter being placed in this unusual position.

The president's and guests' lodgings

The apartments that housed the head of the convent and the guests were not always distinct, for important guests lodged with the abbot or prior, just as a guest at a castle or manor house was entertained in its hall. The creation of a separate establishment for the president and the allocation of special revenues to him, distinct from the common fund set aside for the support of the convent, went back to the days of the Norman kings, and as time went on his duties outside the monastery increased. As the head of a landowning corporation, his administrative responsibilities were those of a feudal lord; he was involved in much journeying to protect and further the material interests of his convent; he had to entertain important visitors on a worthy scale; and now and then he might be required by the King to carry out duties of state. It was essential that the life of his convent should be disturbed as little as possible by these outside activities, and his establishment therefore developed separately.

In fact the accommodation required by an abbot was the same as that of any other lord, lay or ecclesiastical, and the design of his lodgings and of monastic guest houses played as important a part in the development of civil architecture as did the comparable halls and chambers within the medieval castle, for the abbots of great monasteries were patrons of architecture on a larger scale than any of the King's subjects except great nobles and bishops.

When the lodging was on the first floor of the cellarer's range, it generally consisted of a hall, chamber or chambers, and a chapel (Figure 25, i). A simple variation was the addition to this of a single wing projecting westwards at the end of the range nearest the church, as at Chester and Castle Acre (Figure 25, ii), both examples illustrating the very common practice of placing the chapel above the outer parlour. In a great abbey like Westminster (Figure 25, iii), the president's house might grow to a considerable size and bound two or more sides of a courtyard based on the cellarer's range, the upper floor of which might then be used for guests, as at Peterborough.

There was, however, no fixed position for the rooms occupied by the president and guests. At Norwich the cellarer's range housed the guests and also had chambers for the visiting priors of dependent houses, while the bishop's palace grew into an irregular group of buildings north of the church. At Easby the abbot's lodging was also north of the church, and at Kirklees the prioress occupied a building at the north-west angle of the nave. The abbot of Haughmond lived to the south of the claustral buildings, while the priors of Lindisfarne (Figure 25, iv) and Tynemouth (Figure 3) had lodgings near the south end of the dorter range, and the prior of Bolton transferred his house to that position from the cellarer's range in the fourteenth century. It was not uncommon for an old suite of rooms to be abandoned for a new one; this happened on no fewer than three occasions at Bury St Edmunds. In some monasteries the need to provide adequate lodgings for an abbot who had resigned also complicated matters; at Easby in 1311 three ex-abbots were still alive in addition to the presiding one.

The resemblance of an abbot's house or a guest house to a secular manor house is particularly clear when it formed a free-standing building and its plan was not influenced by the necessity of attaching it to the claustral buildings. The priors of Kirkham and Finchale (Figure 29) each had a detached house to the south-east of the cloister, and this was the most favoured position in Cistercian abbeys, where the cellarer's range could not be pressed into service because of its use by the lay brethren.

Early Cistercian custom required the abbot to sleep in the dorter but, within a century of the foundation of most of the English and Welsh houses of the Order, no more than lip-service was being paid to this requirement, and the abbot often had his lodging beyond the east end of the reredorter, through which he remained technically in touch with the dorter. The very early house at Kirkstall is in this position, and so was the lodging of the abbot of Fountains. Even this tenuous connection with the dorter was soon severed, and free-standing houses appear at Croxden (Figure 24, iii) with a ground-floor hall and first-floor chamber, and at Netley (Figure 24, ii) with a first-floor hall and small wings containing chamber and chapel. The fourteenth-century house of the abbots of Roche (Figure 15), with hall, chambers, screens, buttery, pantry and kitchen, is an example of straight-forward domestic planning as advanced as any secular building of its period.

When the guest house was a separate building, it usually stood in the outer court, and two early examples remain at Fountains (Figure 24, i) which illustrate a simple type of plan. Each was of two storeys, with traces of division into two rooms of unequal size, presumably hall and chamber, on each storey, the chambers having garderobes attached. The guest houses at Kirkstall (Figure 24, iv) and Bardney had aisled halls with cross-wings containing chambers, and Kirkstall in its last stage of development (Figure 24, v) with kitchen, service quarters and stables grouped round a small courtyard, was a perfect example of a self-contained domestic establishment of moderate size.

In the later Middle Ages the president's house grew in size and complexity. The magnificent range of halls and chambers south of the claustral buildings at Ely (Figure 2) contained the prior's private lodging on the east, communicating on the west with a series of state apartments that gave complete elasticity to his arrangements for accommodating guests varying in number and rank. At the dissolution, the abbot of Gloucester's house, with similar functions to perform, had two halls, two dining chambers, two kitchens, four butteries, four pantries, a court room, thirteen other chambers, two galleries, a chapel and various cellars and storehouses. It was clearly capable of affording lodging on a princely scale to all comers.

The farmery and little cloister

The farmery (infirmary) generally lay east of the cloister, away from the noise of the outer court. Here the sick monks were cared for, and here lived the very aged for whom the daily routine of life in the cloister was too severe.

The essential parts of a farmery were its hall and chapel, and it usually had its own kitchen to provide more delicate and nourishing food than the normal monastic diet, and sometimes a special frater called the *misericord* in which it was permitted to eat meat. There were also one or two rooms for the obedientiary known as the infirmarer or master of the farmery, who had charge of the estab-lishment.

As a monastic farmery served much the same purpose as a medi-eval hospital, it was arranged on much the same lines, and during the twelfth century the farmeries of the black monks resembled in

Plate 10   CLEEVE ABBEY; THE GATEHOUSE

plan a church with aisled nave and aisled or aisleless chancel. The "nave" of the building was the hall, the beds of the inmates being ranged in the aisles, and the "chancel" was the farmery chapel. Great houses like Ely and Peterborough had farmeries of this type on the grandest possible scale, correctly orientated, and with chapels possessing structural nave and chancel. The farmery at Canterbury cathedral-monastery (Figure 26, i), measuring 237ft (72.2m) from east to west, was as long as many abbey churches of the second rank.

Less grandiose were the farmeries of Norwich and St Augustine's, Canterbury (Figure 26, ii), the halls of which had only one aisle. At the latter monastery it was found more convenient to site the hall north and south, with the chapel projecting from its east side, heralding the transition from the old orientated "church" type of plan to the later arrangement in which hall and chapel were not aligned and not necessarily in structural contact with one another. The Cistercians, who in general did not replace their timber farmeries by stone ones until the thirteenth century, provide good examples of this later plan. An early instance was at Waverley (Figure 26, iii) where the farmery buildings were placed round a small cloister of their own, with a north-south hall on the west side, a chapel on the north, a house perhaps for the infirmarer on the east, and a kitchen on the south. The most impressive example was at Fountains (Figure 27, i) where the vast aisled hall was 180ft long by 80ft wide (54.9 by 24.4m) and, in addition to the chapel, the kitchen and rooms for the infirmarer lay to the east.

The farmery naturally attracted to itself other rooms associated with the physical health of the convent. The monks followed the medieval practice of being bled periodically for reasons of health, and at Norwich the chamber set aside for this purpose was in the farmery, while in most of the Orders a monk who had just been bled was allowed a short period to recuperate on farmery diet. At both the Benedictine monasteries in Canterbury, the baths were also placed near the farmery.

The richer diet of the farmery kitchen may also have been the magnet that drew obedientiaries to this part of the precinct. In the later Middle Ages the Ely, Durham and Bardney obedientiaries had chambers near the farmery, and more than one abbot of Meaux built himself a house near, or appropriated rooms in the farmery in expectation of his retirement.

Quite apart from these additions, the planning of later farmeries was by no means uniform. Furness (Figure 27, ii) and Jervaulx had aisleless but orientated halls, essentially reversions to the early plan, and Thetford (Figure 12) had a series of small chambers

ranged along three sides of a diminutive cloister, the fourth side
housing the hall and chapel. Often, as a result of gradual development, the farmery came to share a little cloister of this sort with
other buildings; at Rievaulx and Tintern with the dorter range and
the reredorter. Premonstratensian farmeries appear to be exceptional in that only one has been found to possess a chapel.

Sometimes the lie of the land made it impossible to place the
farmery east of the claustral buildings. At Furness it lay south of
the frater, and at Easby an elaborate group of buildings extending
north from the church housed both abbot and farmery, providing
an unusual and effective visual balance to the cloister on the south
side of the nave.

The larger Cistercian monasteries had farmeries for their lay
brethren, generally in the form of an aisled hall with a north–south
axis, placed, as at Jervaulx and Roche (Figure 15), near the lay
brethren's reredorter.

The outer court

The other buildings necessary for the efficient running of a monastery lay in the outer court, between the cloister and the main
entrance to the precinct (Figures 2 and 3). Their number and
purpose varied according to the size of the convent, and their
position in relation to the church according to the demands of
the site. Wherever possible, the outer court was west of the church,
so that laymen, who were admitted to this part of the precinct in the
houses of all the Orders, could have direct access to the nave, and
so that provisions could conveniently be brought into the cellarer's
range.

When the *lodgings for guests* were not directly associated with
the president's house or placed on the upper floor of the cellarer's
range, a separate house was usually built for them in the outer
court. Examples at Fountains and Kirkstall have been mentioned,
and there are others at Monk Bretton and Furness.

Most of the other buildings in the court might often be timber-
framed, and survivals are comparatively rare. An idea of their
number and variety, however, can be gained from the fact that
the precinct of the small priory of Nunkeeling contained five barns
for different types of grain, a malthouse, a mill, a slaughter house,
a pigsty, separate sheds for oxen, cows and calves, two stables,
a smithy, a henhouse and a dovecot. At Canterbury cathedral-
monastery and at Fountains brewhouses and bakehouses remain,
and at Fountains the abbey mill still survives. At Boxley a long
two-storied building was probably intended partly for storage and
partly for administrative offices. At Glastonbury the great barn still

serves its original purpose. Great monasteries like Norwich might have a permanent masons' lodge, carpenters' shop and drawing office, and Tynemouth (Figure 3) had a special workshop for the plumber. Foundations of many buildings are exposed in the outer court at Tintern.

In addition to all these buildings there was an *almonry* close to the gateway of the precinct and, where the gatehouse has survived, traces of the destroyed buildings of the almonry can sometimes be seen on its walls, as at Kirkham and Thetford. Here alms were distributed to the poor and sick of the neighbourhood by an obedientiary called the almoner, and in many of the great houses groups of pensioners were maintained by the convent. The twelfth-century stairway that is a notable feature of the domestic buildings of Canterbury cathedral-monastery belonged to a hall known as the North Hall, which adjoined the almonry and which has been aptly described as a casual ward for poor or destitute wayfarers. Monastic schools were also placed near the gate.

The main gatehouse through which the precinct was entered, whether small and simple or large and ostentatious, was generally not less than two storeys high. The ground floor was pierced by a broad gate-passage with an archway at either end of the building. The usual medieval plan reserved this broad arch for wheeled traffic and provided a small arch beside it for pedestrians. The two arches were often in a cross-wall in the middle of the gate-passage, as at Easby (Figure 28, iii) and Worksop, but the practice was not uniform; at Battle they are at one end of the passage only, St Osyth's has a large arch with a small one on each side of it, and several gatehouses, of which Thetford (Figure 28, i) and the two examples at Bury St Edmunds are good instances, simply had the broad arch with no special provision for pedestrians. A doorway in one of the side walls of the gate-passage led to the room used by the porter, who kept the gate and controlled traffic entering and leaving the monastery.

Gatehouses vary in size from the small gabled building at Kingswood to the massive and magnificent examples at St Albans and Thornton (Figure 28, ii). Their upper floors had various uses. At York and Whalley the upper floor was a chapel, but the largest gatehouses were more often put to administrative uses; those at St Albans and Ely contained prisons, and the latter had a court room as well. Prisons in this position were for layfolk who came within the territorial jurisdiction of the abbot as feudal lord, but the series of small and comfortless cells in the basement of the abbot's

Plate 11   THORNTON ABBEY; THE GATEHOUSE

house at Fountains, each with its own garderobe and floor-staple for the prisoner's shackles, was intended for recalcitrant monks.

When the precinct was extensive, more than one gatehouse was needed. Bury St Edmunds had four, of which the Great Gate and St James's Gate have survived, and there was also a separate gate to the vineyards. St Augustine's, Canterbury, retains two fine specimens. York had a watergate leading to the quays alongside the Ouse, as did Tintern on the Wye, and Furness, besides having two gatehouses on the line of the precinct, had a third in advance of it, giving access to the small courtyard outside the main gate usually found in Cistercian abbeys, and a fourth within the precinct leading to the cemetery.

In the great monasteries it was not uncommon for the outer court to be divided by buildings extending westwards from the cellarer's range. The northern part then served as the outer court proper, with direct access from the main gatehouse to the church, and the southern part, entered through a subsidiary gatehouse in the dividing screen of buildings, was generally an inner court associated with the president's lodging. Subsidiary gatehouses serving this particular purpose can be seen at Peterborough and Reading.

In a number of monasteries, especially those of the black monks, *parish churches* were found on or close to the line of the precinct. Sometimes, as in the case of St Olave's Church near the west gatehouse of York, they were of earlier foundation than the monastery itself. At Bury St Edmunds, however, one was the successor of an old parish church that had been demolished to make way for extensions to the monastery. At both Reading and Abingdon a church adjoins the western gatehouse of the abbey, and in each case there was a hospital or lay farmery dedicated to St John the Baptist close to it, administered by the abbey.

Cistercian abbeys, the naves of which were used by the lay brethren and were therefore not parochial, provided a special *chapel for layfolk* in a courtyard outside the main gatehouse. There are examples at Kirkstead and Furness, while at Merevale and Tilty these chapels have survived through becoming parish churches after the dissolution.

The precinct was surrounded by a wall which, although often high and well built, was rarely capable of serious defence. York and Ewenny with their battlements and towers are exceptions, and at Tynemouth (Figure 3) the priory stands within the walls of a castle, and its precinct is entered through a keep-gatehouse built late in the fourteenth century. The more usual type of precinct wall with a plain coping can be seen at Furness and Fountains.

Buildings outside the precinct

The provisioning of a religious house and the efficient administration of its outlying estates required buildings and earthworks that can often be recognised far from the mother-house. A plentiful supply of fish was essential for the monastic diet, and wherever possible the monks secured fishing rights in rivers and lakes. Titchfield had rights on the Meon down to the Solent, and St Dogmael's on the Teifi, while Chester not only maintained a boat on the Dee but also had a ship and ten nets off Anglesey. The fishing rights in the great mere of Skipsea were the subject of a dispute between York and Meaux which ended in trial by battle, and for the better exploitation of its rights in the Somerset marshes Glastonbury built the small fish-house at Meare, a fourteenth-century building that still stands.

In addition to their rights in natural waters, the monasteries followed the normal medieval practice of constructing and stocking artificial *fishponds* and hatcheries in or close to their precincts. The earthworks of these are often recognisable, even when dry, and particularly fine sets remain near Fountains and Thornton.

The *granges* or farms of the black monks varied greatly in size and had no standard pattern. The largest, like Minster-in-Thanet, were almost monasteries in miniature; others, especially in the later Middle Ages, were given specialised functions as dairy, arable or sheep farms. The abbots of the greater houses often used particular estates as country retreats, and built themselves substantial houses. Parts of two such remain in Cheshire, both once belonging to the abbots of Chester; at Saighton in the fertile land between Gowy and Dee, and at Ince on the bleak southern shore of the Mersey estuary.

The *barns* in which the various types of grain were stored within the precinct for the immediate use of the convent have already been mentioned, and up and down the countryside can be seen other barns into which was gathered the produce of the outlying estates. The great barn at Bradford-on-Avon (Figure 28, iv) served Shaftesbury, and the barn at Enstone bears an inscription recording that it was built by the abbot of Winchcombe at the instance of his bailiff there.

So long as the lay brethren remained a living force among the Cistercians, they worked the outlying lands and were quartered in specially constructed granges provided with chapels. No good example of an early Cistercian grange is known to have survived intact in this country, but at Bewerley in Nidderdale there is a lodge that was remodelled shortly before the dissolution. Where the land was capable of cultivation, the grange was an agricultural centre, but on the desolate fells of the north and the west it served rather as the headquarters of the extensive sheep-runs that were characteristic of the Cistercian economy.

The Cistercian and Grandmontine plans

The early monasteries of the Cistercians in England followed the well-established plan of the black monks except in the form of their churches. This plan has been recovered by excavation at Waverley (Figure 14, i) and traces of it can be seen at Kirkstall, Fountains, and other houses of the Order. From the first, however, the necessity of providing accommodation for numbers of lay brethren made the traditional arrangement of the buildings unsatisfactory, and in the second half of the twelfth century there was added to this a great increase in the number of recruits to the Order and in the wealth of individual houses, providing both reason and means for ambitious rebuilding that extended well into the thirteenth century. It was during this time that a new and easily recognisable plan imposed itself on practically all Cistercian houses with a rigidity that reflected the centralised organisation of the Order.

In the *dorter range* the usual slype was replaced by a room divided into two parts, the western end serving as a library with a doorway to the cloister, and the eastern end as a sacristy with a doorway to the transept. The treasury was usually on the floor above at the head of the night stairs, and was vaulted in stone to protect the contents from fire. The sacrist's bed was at this end of the dorter, where he could keep an eye on the treasury and look after the clock, which was usually in the transept.

The day stairs were moved out of the dorter range to a position at the east end of the frater range, as at Fountains and Neath, and traces of the actual change of plan are visible at Rievaulx and Jervaulx. Inner parlour and slype adjoined one another on the side of the chapter house away from the church, the slype being either a structurally independent passage as at Tintern, or a space partitioned off from the dorter undercroft as at Fountains and Roche (Figure 15). It was often prolonged eastwards as a gallery giving covered access to the farmery, with a branch leading to the eastern arm of the church.

The rest of the dorter undercroft was used as the warming house only in such exceptional abbeys as Basingwerk and Cleeve. In French monasteries it sometimes formed the novices' quarters, but its use is less certain in this country except when, as at Byland and Furness, it originally had open arcades in its main walls and was a workshop associated with the early insistence of the white monks on the importance of manual labour.

Plate 12   *TITCHFIELD ABBEY; THE NAVE CONVERTED INTO THE GATEHOUSE OF A LATER MANSION*

The most characteristic feature of the new plan was the arrangement of the *frater range*. The first Cistercian fraters were sited
parallel to the cloister (Figure 14, i) after the manner of the black
monks, and fraters of this type continued to be built occasionally,
as at Valle Crucis and Cymmer. But the new plan adopted by most
of the houses had the advantage of saving space by siting the frater
at right angles to the cloister and projecting well beyond the main
walls of the range. This gave room for the inclusion of the warming
house and day stairs to the east, and the kitchen to the west of the
frater, all within the main walls of the range and with direct access
to the cloister. Fountains has a noble warming house in this position,
with two great fireplaces in its east wall and a series of vents opposite
to allow warm air to enter the frater. Both there and at Waverley
the space to the south of the warming house was used as a yard
with a wood shed to supply the communal fire.

In its new position, the kitchen could serve the frater of the
monks on one side and the frater of the lay brethren on the other,
for the *cellarer's range* was largely devoted to the latter. As the
ground floor of this range had to house the cellar as well as the
lay brethren's frater, it was often of considerable length and projected well beyond the cloister. Furness of sixteen bays and Byland
of eighteen are both good examples, but Fountains has the most
impressive west range in Europe; 300ft (91.5m) long and vaulted in
twenty-two double bays from a central row of columns, it is a good
instance of a method of building often used for cellarers' ranges,
being built as an open room and divided into its component parts
by partitions. The alternative method is best seen at Rufford,
where structural walls divide the range into a cellar on the north,
an outer parlour in the centre, and the lay brethren's frater on the
south, these being the normal uses to which the ground floor of the
range was put. The first floor was the dorter of the lay brethren,
with its own night stairs to their quire in the structural nave of the
church. Their day stairs were on the cloister side at Byland, and on
the west side at Fountains where they rise above a vaulted room that
served as the cellarer's office. At the end of the range away from the
church there was communication with the reredorter of the lay
brethren, which usually projected to the west.

In a number of Cistercian houses a space called a "lane" was left
between the western alley of the cloister and the lay brethren's
range, perhaps to insulate the cloister from the noise and disturbance
of the more active life of the lay brethren and the work of the cellar.
The lane ran the whole length of the cloister, from which it was
separated by a wall, and passed through the frater range. Varying in
width from a mere passage at Byland (Figure 28, v) to a space as

broad as a road at Kirkstall (Figure 28, vi), it usually had a doorway to the church at one end. The great archways through which it traversed the frater range can be seen at Kirkstall, although the dwindling number of lay brethren in later times caused the dividing wall of the lane to be demolished and its space thrown into the cloister.

The lane is a peculiarity of a monastery with a large number of lay brethren, but there are indications at some continental Cistercian houses that no provision was made for housing the lay brethren in the west range, and at some English houses of the Order that range is inadequate for their needs. Rievaulx is an obvious example, having a remarkably small west range, built at a date when it is known that there were no fewer than 500 lay brethren serving the abbey. Even allowing for those dispersed to the granges, this range must have been inadequate for the community, and the lay brethren probably had separate buildings clear of the cloister, as did early Carthusian lay brethren.

The three English Grandmontine priories of Alberbury, Craswall and Grosmont all inherited distinctive features from the continental houses of their Order (Figure 14, ii). In addition to their characteristic churches, they had chapter houses that did not project beyond the main walls of the dorter range, attaining reasonable dimensions by having their long axis from north to south. Their day stairs, like those of the Cistercians, were placed in the south-east angle of the cloister, but were allowed to project into the cloister alley. As an austere Order influenced by the life of the early hermits, their dorters were from the outset divided into separate cubicles or cells.

Charterhouses, double monasteries and friaries

The Carthusians evolved a plan of their own (Figure 17) which clearly reflects the rigours of their Rule and the centralisation of their Order. In its fullest extension, this plan required the buildings of a charterhouse to be arranged round several courtyards. The first of these, accessible from the outer world through a gatehouse, contained the guest houses, barns, stables, and other offices of a normal outer court, and from it there was access, either direct or more usually through another and smaller court, to the church, to which was attached a diminutive cloister little bigger than a light-well. The chapter house occupied its usual position on the east side of this cloister; it was provided with an altar, and was generally about the same size as the small, aisleless presbytery of the church. At Mount Grace it followed the continental custom of being built against the church without an intervening sacristy.

The church and its little cloister, with other buildings that included the frater and the prior's cell, separated the outer court from the great cloister around which the individual cells of the monks were placed. Each of these was a small house with a workroom, bedroom and oratory, and each stood within a walled garden, with its own garderobe. The cloister wall of each cell had an L-shaped hatch through which food could be passed to the monk without the server being seen, for meals in common were taken in the frater only on certain days.

Like other austere Orders, the Carthusians had lay brethren to ensure the complete seclusion of the monks by performing the heavy work of the house. So far as their duties allowed, the life of the lay brethren was modelled on that of the monks and, although in the early houses of the Order they had a separate establishment connected to the great cloister by a through passage, in the later houses their cells were placed round another cloister within the main precinct, sited to give access on the one hand to the church and on the other to the outer court where much of their work lay.

Some of these special features of Carthusian planning survive in the London Charterhouse, where there are remains of the doorways and service hatches of the cells, and where the lay brethren's cloister survives in the plan of Wash House Court, and at Hinton where there is a chapter house in perfect preservation and where excavation has recently revealed the plan of the great and small cloisters. But Mount Grace provides by far the most complete example in the country for the study of practically all these distinctive arrangements.

In the double houses of Gilbertines and Bridgettines the problem to be solved was not the creation of individual cells for members of the convent, but the planning of what was in effect a single precinct containing a monastery and a nunnery.

The plan of only one double Gilbertine house is known in its entirety—that of Watton in Humberside (Figure 18). The solution adopted there was the simple one of having two complete sets of conventual buildings, each with its own church, cloister, chapter house, dorter and offices. The nuns' church was larger than that of the canons, and was divided longitudinally by a wall, thereby enabling the nuns in one half of the church to hear the services conducted by the canons in the other half. The two sets of conventual buildings were connected by a long passage in which was set a "turning window" through which it was possible for the members of the two communities to speak to one another.

A different solution was favoured by the Bridgettines, who had a single church with the conventual buildings of the nuns on one side and those of the canons on the other. Segregation in the church itself was ensured by having the altars served by the canons at ground-floor level, while the nuns occupied first-floor galleries round the walls on a similar principle to the first-floor quires of the Cistercian nunneries in Germany.

The remains of England's only Bridgettine house, incorporated in the basement of the present Syon House, are too scanty to be identified with certainty, but may have formed part of the vaulted undercroft of a long range belonging to the nuns or canons, placed at right angles to the vanished church, for this Order rarely placed its buildings round a cloister.

As might be expected, the arrangements of the houses of friars differed from those of the monasteries of the older Orders, for their purpose—as a base of operations and missionary head-quarters rather than a permanent home—was not the same. The friars were mostly settled in towns, and were late-comers to the scene, so that they often had to be content with inconvenient and restricted sites that gave them little scope for regularity in setting out their buildings. They are found tucked into the south-east angle of the city of Lincoln, and occupying land formerly used as gardens within the west wall of the city of Chester.

When they could, they arranged their buildings round a cloister, fragmentary examples of which remain at Coventry Carmelites and Great Yarmouth Franciscans, and the chapter house and dorter generally occupied their traditional positions in the east range. But the frater is sometimes found in the west range, as at Canterbury Dominicans. At Gloucester Dominicans the south range, which would have contained the frater in a monastery of the older Orders, housed the "studies," a long room with wall-recesses to serve as carrells and provision for a library, and there is little doubt that the emphasis placed by the friars on learning must have left similar marks, as at Clare (Figure 21), on others of their houses.

Distinctive features of the plans of friaries were the occasional separation of the cloister from the church by a space like a lane, as at Norwich Dominicans (Figure 19) and Walsingham Franciscans (Figure 20), and the practice, already mentioned, of allowing the first-floor rooms of the main ranges to project over the cloister alleys. Friaries were celebrated for their conduits of running water, which in some cases were shared by the towns in which they were established.

The disintegration of the medieval plan

Monastic plans did not remain unchanged throughout the Middle
Ages. The greater monasteries of the twelfth and thirteenth
centuries had been in the forefront of European architecture, and
their buildings provided the monks with living conditions that were
as good as, and in the matter of sanitation usually better than, those
of their lay contemporaries. By later medieval standards these
conditions were poor, and the monks were to some extent prevented
from keeping abreast of the times by the great legacy of buildings
they had inherited from earlier centuries, and by the fact that practically no convent could shoulder the financial burden of complete
replanning when the tide of benefactions had begun to ebb.

General chapters and reforming bishops, in trying to restore the
observance of the Rule to its primitive purity, found that this
entailed, often enough, an incidental attempt to re-impose a
twelfth-century standard of living. The monks, on their part,
compiled sets of "customs" in which the traditional interpretation
of the Rule peculiar to individual houses or groups of houses
was set out, and these became a means of recording and giving
local sanction to minor departures from the Rule's strictness.
When Pope Benedict XII issued new constitutions to the Benedictines, Cistercians and Augustinians between 1335 and 1339 a
widespread change had already begun to leave its mark on monastic
buildings in general, and it is recognisable not only in the design
of new buildings but also in the conversion of old ones to new uses.
Many factors contributed to it, including an increased emphasis
on the value of a university education in monastic life, the growing
importance of the president's establishment in relation to the rest
of the convent, the reduced number of brethren in many houses and,
above all, a general desire for better standards of material comfort
and privacy.

The changes can be seen most easily among the Cistercians,
because they had started with a more uniform plan than the other
Orders. The gradual abandonment of the features that had distinguished the life of the white monks from the black was reflected
in the abandonment of the distinctive Cistercian type of frater.
At Whalley, where the slow building campaign did not reach the
frater until the fifteenth century, it was built on an east to west
axis. At Croxden there is evidence for the abandonment of that part
of the frater projecting beyond the main range, while the best
example is at Cleeve where a ground-floor frater sited north and
south was replaced by a fine first-floor hall sited east and west.
The general introduction of a meat diet brought with it an extended
use of the misericord and the meat kitchen, previously reserved to

the farmery; Jervaulx built a new misericord adjoining its frater, and the division of the frater at Kirkstall into two storeys may have been for the same purpose.

The use of the room next to the transept partly as a sacristy and partly as a library was also discontinued, and it became a through passage as in the houses of other Orders. Special provision, apart from the old book cupboards and closets, began to be made for libraries.

After the fourteenth century the disappearance of the lay brethren increased the similarity of the Cistercian and Benedictine plans by enabling the abbots of Hailes and Salley to transfer their lodgings to the cellarer's range, and the abbot of Forde to use that range as the starting point for a most ambitious house. Most Cistercian abbots, however, already possessed adequate lodgings east of the claustral buildings, and the buildings formerly occupied by the lay brethren could be made to serve other purposes. At Wykeham the first floor became a granary, as it also did at Rievaulx where the ground floor was divided into a series of small chambers with fireplaces, in the interests of comfort and privacy.

This creation of private chambers was common to many of the Orders and affected many parts of their houses. It had become customary to allow obedientiaries and scholars to have their own rooms, and the claims of retired abbots and corrodians had also to be considered. Most of the conversion of buildings into small chambers was carried out in the fourteenth and fifteenth centuries, a good instance being the dorter undercroft at Byland, while the plan of the small Benedictine nunnery at Wilberfoss (Figure 30) provides an extreme example. At the same time, dorters were being divided by wainscot partitions into separate bedchambers, and the aisles of farmery halls were also being cut up to provide wards and apartments, as at Fountains and Tintern.

The multiplicity of rooms with fireplaces robbed the communal fire of its significance in the life of the convent. The warming house ceased to be used simply as a place for restoring warmth to chilled limbs on a winter's day, and became a common room where informal meetings and celebrations might be held, and where at Durham a cask of wine might grace the proceedings. One of the two great communal fireplaces at Fountains was blocked up, and at Forde an early sixteenth-century reconstruction abolished the warming house altogether and replaced it by a passage. At Rievaulx the change was even more significant, for the warming house there was converted to domestic uses and equipped with sinks and draining floors.

The invasion of the claustral buildings by the domestic services was widespread in small monasteries and nunneries. Cool parlours and slypes on the ground floor lent themselves readily to use for storage. At the time of the dissolution Kirklees had a bread house in this position, Thicket and Yedingham had brewhouses giving on to the cloister, Baysdale and Wilberfoss (Figure 30) had dairies next to the chapter house, and Rievaulx used the undercrofts of both dorter and frater for tanning hides.

If the lower floors were capable of being adapted in this way, the dry upper floors were excellent for the storage of grain. It has already been seen that the upper floor of the cellarer's range at Rievaulx became a barn, but at the smaller houses of Handale and Thicket the conversion was more drastic and by the early sixteenth century the fraters themselves were being used as granaries. There can be little doubt that in these cases the convent was dining in private chambers or at the president's table.

This state of affairs was not uncommon in small houses, and was often due to the fact that the increase in the size and complexity of the president's establishment went hand in hand with a reduction in the numbers of the convent. There are indications that, well before the close of the Middle Ages, a solution was being sought to this problem by making the abbot or prior's establishment the centre of the life of a reduced convent.

At Finchale (Figure 29, ii–iii), which became little more than a centre for rest and relaxation to which the mother-house of Durham sent those of its monks who needed a change, an extensive prior's lodging was built east of the claustral buildings, the adjacent parts of which were later converted to serve it. Part of the frater was divided into chambers, so that the convent took its meals at the prior's table. At Lindisfarne (Figure 24, iv) on the other hand, the frater was converted into a hall of secular design with dais, bay window and central hearth, communicating on the east with a ground-floor common room for the convent and a first-floor chamber for the prior, while its screens passage on the west was entered through a porch from the outer court, and the cellarer's range was cut up to house its pantry and buttery. A late rebuilding of the frater range at the substantial abbey of Muchelney shows a somewhat similar arrangement, except that the alternative plan of placing the abbot's chamber over the screens, with access through them to the frater, was adopted. The prior of Lindisfarne and the abbot of Muchelney were, in fact, using the fraters as their great halls.

Policies of retrenchment like these preserved communal life so far as taking meals was concerned, and in this respect contrasted with another policy adopted in some houses, especially those of larger size. This was the division of the convent into a number of separate households, often with separate kitchens. It appears on a small scale at Bardney in the fifteenth century, the sixteen monks of the convent forming three households taking their meals in the abbot's hall, the frater and the farmery.

The late arrangement of monastic buildings, and especially the multiplication and placing of kitchens, suggests a similar state of affairs in other houses, and sometimes shows which departments were being grouped to form a unit for provisioning and accounting. At Kirkham, for instance, one kitchen is placed to serve the farmery, misericord and prior's lodging, and a second kitchen served the frater and the guest house. In a great cathedral-monastery like Ely, not only the bishop and the prior but also seven obedientiaries had separate quarters, and four of them had their own kitchens.

The disintegration of the old plan reached its most extreme form in a few houses where the most characteristic feature of a medieval monastery—the cloister—was abandoned. The early sixteenth-century reconstruction of the cloister at Forde was done in a manner which shows that it no longer served its old purpose, and the conversion of the frater at Lindisfarne involved the abandonment of the cloister alleys. At Valle Crucis the eastern alley was blocked by the external stairs to a hall and chamber the abbot made for himself by appropriating the northern end of the dorter.

The Renaissance and the dissolution

By the early sixteenth century the medieval monastic plan had therefore outlived some of its usefulness, and only the accident of the dissolution prevented this from becoming as clear in England and Wales as it did on the Continent. In 1540 only the first signs of Renaissance taste in architecture had reached this side of the Channel, expressing themselves in a hesitant liking for "antique" ornament. The monks were as ready as anyone to approve the new fashion. It appears in tomb design at Boxgrove and Thetford, on panelling at Thame, and in architectural ornament at Forde. But the general effect of the Renaissance on planning and elevational design was still to be felt.

At Bath alone, the complete rebuilding of the abbey church in the first forty years of the century gave a hint of the shape of things to come. The new church was traditional in design and small in size, occupying only the site of the nave of its Norman predecessor and constituting an acknowledgement that the numbers of the convent had dropped to half their twelfth-century level. The same acknowledgement can be seen in makeshift arrangements at Talley, Finchale (Figure 29, iii) and Creake. The significance of Bath is that the new church was designed from the first as a free-standing building except where the old cellarer's range abutted on it. The conventional relationship with the cloister was sacrificed, no provision was made for a cloister alley along the south walls of the nave where a modern alley now stands, and no provision was made for a dorter range to join the transept.

The full impact of the Renaissance on monastic planning can only be followed on the Continent. In England and Wales an abrupt end was put to this development by the dissolution.

A few churches, such as Peterborough and Gloucester, were preserved as new cathedral foundations. Parts of many others, such as the nave of Bridlington and the north aisle of Crowland, survived because they were serving as parish churches, and in a few cases the parish had the means and the courage to acquire the whole monastic church, as at Selby and Tewkesbury. Some, like Titchfield and Netley, were converted into great houses. But the majority, passing into lay hands, were wholly or partly demolished for the sake of their materials. Building materials, fragments of which can be recognised at Deal and Yarmouth, also went to the new artillery forts that were being erected along the south coast; and in the west, stone and timber from Conwy Abbey and Bangor Friary were shipped to Caernarfon and used to repair the royal buildings there.

The excavation of monastic sites reveals from time to time evidence of the wholesale destruction that attended the dissolution. Improvised furnaces at Croxden, Monk Bretton and elsewhere show how the lead from roofs and windows was melted down for dispatch to the King, to whom its use and the use of precious metals were reserved. At Roche the quire stalls were used as fuel for these lead furnaces, and the remaining woodwork and fittings were sold piecemeal. Layers of masons' chippings and fragments of discarded sculpture show how the cloister at Thornton was pressed into service as a breaker's yard. Where demolition was neither so deliberate nor so thorough, the roofless walls became in time a convenient source of building stone for neighbouring farms and villages.

Plans

The key to the plans can be found after Figure 30

With the exception of Figures 2 and 3, all plans are reproduced to one or other of two scales for ease of comparison. Plans of churches and complete monasteries are to the scale of 1:1200 (Figures 4–22 and 29); individual features and small buildings are to the scale of 1: 800 (Figures 1, 23–8 and 30).

The following figures are based on more detailed published plans by courtesy of: the Cambridge University Press (2); the Chester and North Wales Architectural, Archaeological and Historic Society (11); P G M Dickinson (21); F C Elliston-Erwood (19); the Governors of the Charterhouse, Professor W F Grimes, and Messrs. Longmans, Green & Co Ltd (6, v; 9, ii); A R Martin (6, iii; 9, iii; 20); the Royal Archaeological Institute of Great Britain and Ireland (6, ii, iv; 18; 25, i); the Royal Commission on Historical Monuments (England) (4, iii; 5, i, ii; 22, vii; 24, iii); the Society of Antiquaries of London (6, i, viii; 13, ii; 14, ii; 16); the Surrey Archaeological Society (14, i; 25, iii); the Thoresby Society (23, iv, v; 27, vi); the Victoria History of the Counties of England (2; 9, i); the Yorkshire Archaeological Society (7, iii; 10, i, ii; 22, v; 23, i; 26, i); the Yorkshire Philosophical Society (8, i; 22, iv).

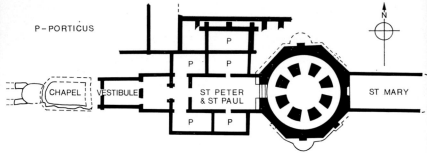

St Peter and St Paul, Canterbury (Saxon)

P – PORTICUS

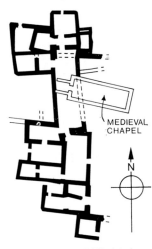

MEDIEVAL CHAPEL

Tintagel (Celtic)

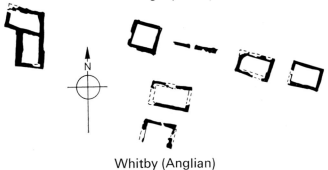

Whitby (Anglian)

0	15	30
Metres		

0	50	100
Feet		

Fig 1   Pre-Conquest monasteries

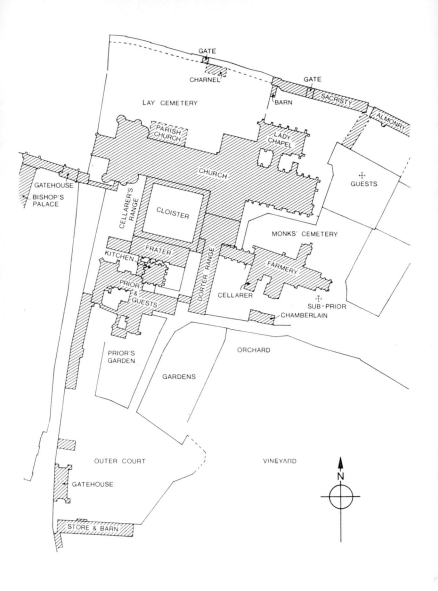

GATE

CHARNEL

GATE

LAY CEMETERY

BARN

SACRISTY

ALMONRY

PARISH CHURCH

LADY CHAPEL

CHURCH

GATEHOUSE

GUESTS

BISHOP'S PALACE

CELLARER'S RANGE

CLOISTER

MONKS' CEMETERY

FRATER

KITCHEN

DORTER RANGE

FARMERY

PRIOR & GUESTS

CELLARER

SUB-PRIOR

CHAMBERLAIN

PRIOR'S GARDEN

ORCHARD

GARDENS

OUTER COURT

VINEYARD

N

GATEHOUSE

STORE & BARN

15 0 15 30 45 60 75 90
Metres

50 0 50 100 150 200 250 300
Feet

Fig 2 Ely
The precinct of a cathedral-monastery

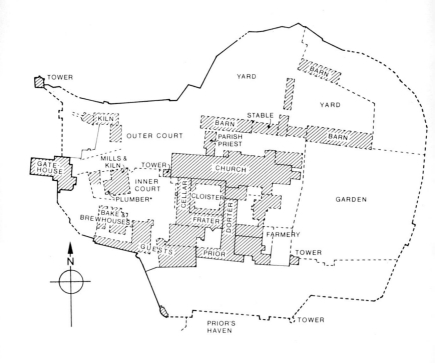

| 15 | 0 | 15 | 30 | 45 | 60 | 75 | 90 |
Metres

| 50 | 0 | 50 | 100 | 150 | 200 | 250 | 300 |
Feet

Fig 3   Tynemouth Priory
A monastic precinct within a castle

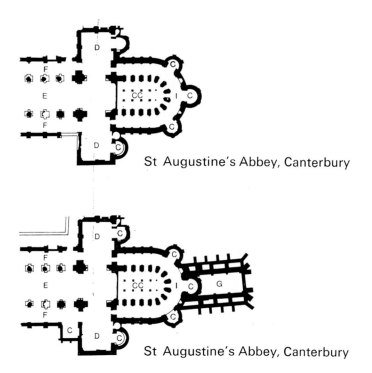

St Augustine's Abbey, Canterbury

St Augustine's Abbey, Canterbury

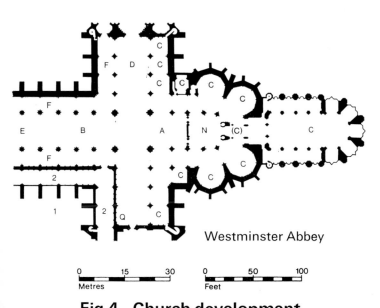

Westminster Abbey

0   15   30   0   50   100
Metres   Feet

Fig 4 Church development
The apse and ambulatory, and the chevet

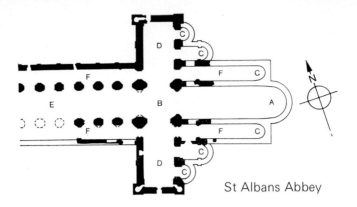

St Albans Abbey

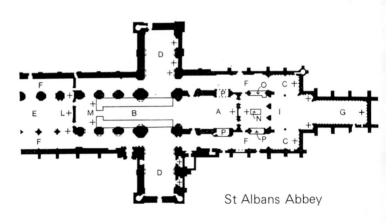

St Albans Abbey

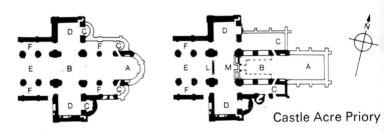

Castle Acre Priory

Metres | Feet

Fig 5   Church development

Parallel apses and their replacement

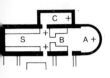

Grosmont Priory
(Grandmontine)

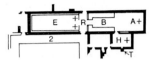

Hulne Friary (Carmelite)

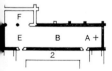

Lincoln Friary (Franciscan)

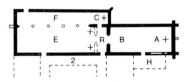

Brecon Friary (Dominican)

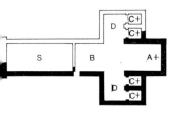

London Charterhouse
(Carthusian)

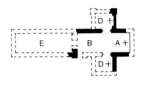

Haughmond Abbey, the
early church (Augustinian)

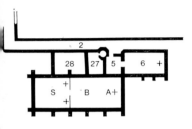

Tintern Abbey (Cistercian),
the early church

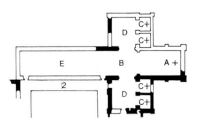

Torre Abbey
(Premonstratensian)

Fig 6 Church development
Austere planning

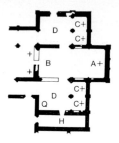

Valle Crucis Abbey

Byland Abbey

Jervaulx Abbey

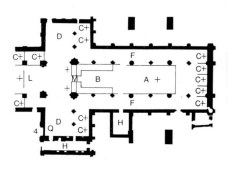

Rievaulx Abbey

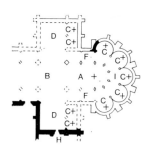

Croxden Abbey

0   15   30
Metres

0   50   100
Feet

Fig 7 Church development
The Cistercians

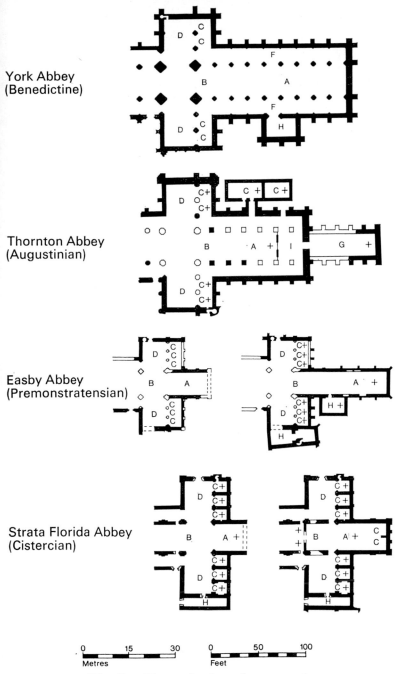

York Abbey
(Benedictine)

Thornton Abbey
(Augustinian)

Easby Abbey
(Premonstratensian)

Strata Florida Abbey
(Cistercian)

0   15   30
Metres

0   50   100
Feet

Fig 8   Church development

Extended presbyteries

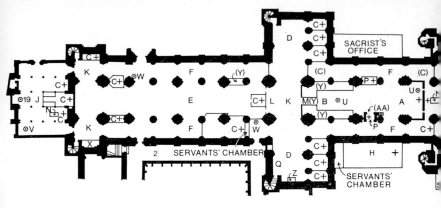

Durham cathedral-monastery (Benedict[...])

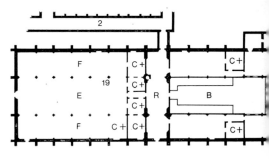

London Charterhouse (Carthusian)

London Franciscan Friary

| 0 | 15 | 30 |
Metres

| 0 | 50 |
Feet

Fig 9   Ritual arrangements

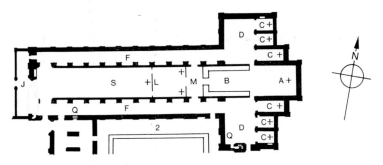

Fountains Abbey (twelfth century)

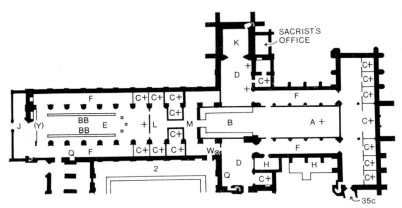

Fountains Abbey (early sixteenth century)

Fig 10 Cistercian ritual arrangements

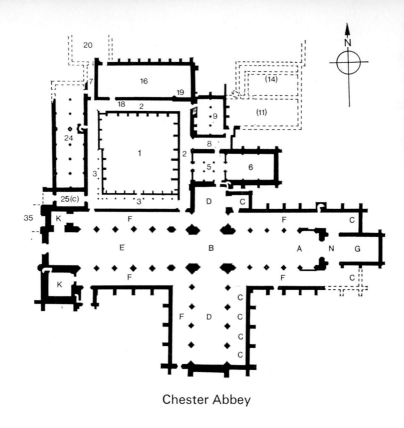

Chester Abbey

| Metres | 0 | 15 | 30 |
| Feet | 0 | 50 | 100 |

Fig 11 A Benedictine plan

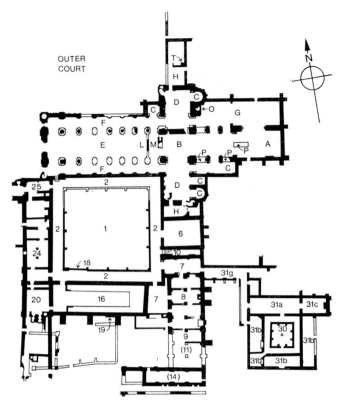

OUTER
COURT

Thetford Priory

0   15   30   0   50   100
Metres   Feet

Fig 12   A Cluniac plan

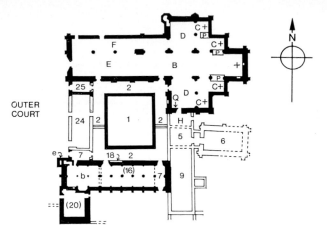

Lanercost Priory (canons)

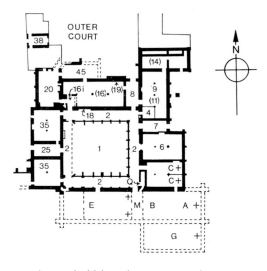

Lacock Abbey (canonesses)

Metres 0 15 30

Feet 0 50 100

Fig 13 Augustinian plans

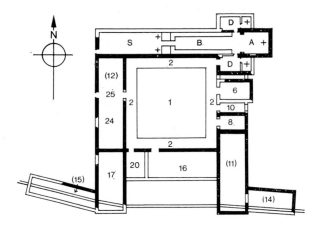

Waverley Abbey (Cistercian)

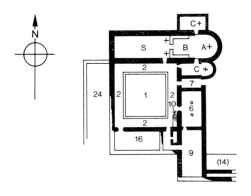

Craswall Priory (Grandmontine)

Fig 14   Early Cistercian and Grandmontine plans

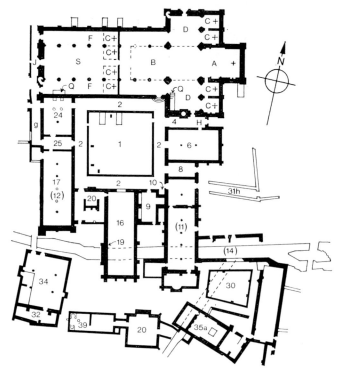

Roche Abbey

| 0 | 15 | 30 |
| Metres | | |

| 0 | 50 | 100 |
| Feet | | |

Fig 15 A mature Cistercian plan

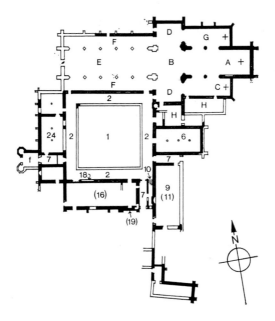

Leiston Abbey

Fig 16 A Premonstratensian plan

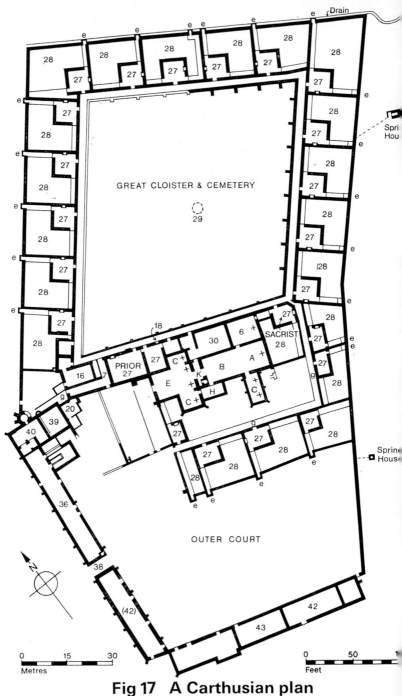

Fig 17 A Carthusian plan

Mount Grace Charterhouse

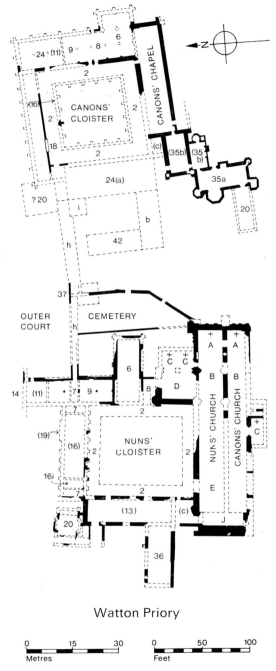

CANONS' CHAPEL

CANONS' CLOISTER

OUTER COURT

CEMETERY

NUNS' CLOISTER

NUNS' CHURCH

CANONS' CHURCH

Watton Priory

| 0 | 15 | 30 |
Metres

| 0 | 50 | 100 |
Feet

Fig 18 A Gilbertine plan

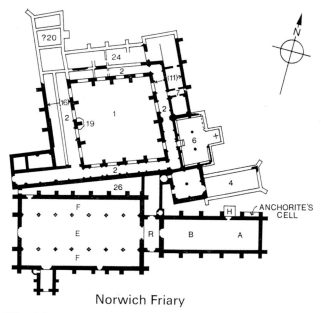

Norwich Friary

Fig 19   A Dominican plan in a city

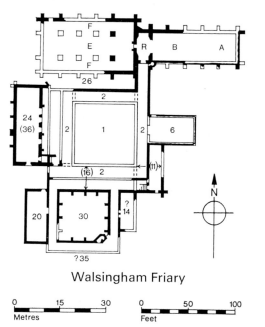

Walsingham Friary

0   15   30   0   50   100
Metres   Feet

Fig 20   A Franciscan plan in the country

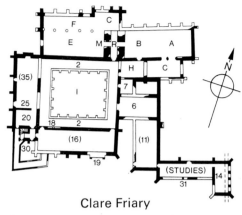

Clare Friary

Fig 21   An Augustinian friars' plan

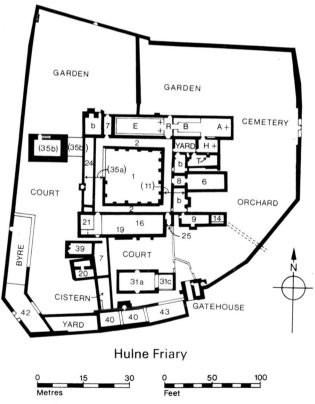

Hulne Friary

Metres 0 15 30

Feet 0 50 100

Fig 22   A Carmelite plan

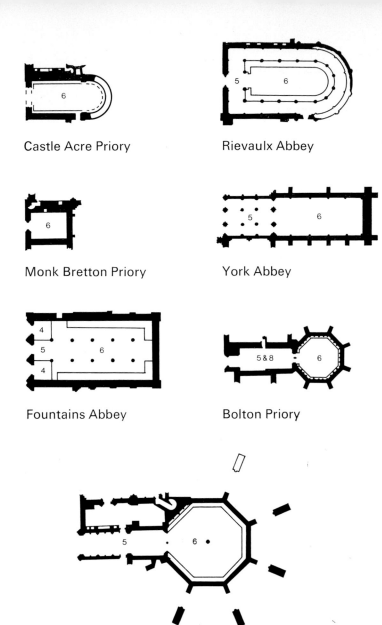

Castle Acre Priory

Rievaulx Abbey

Monk Bretton Priory

York Abbey

Fountains Abbey

Bolton Priory

Westminster Abbey

Metres 0 15 30

Feet 0 50 100

Fig 23 Chapter houses

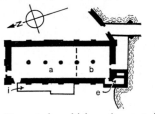

Fountains Abbey (guests)

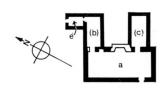

Netley Abbey (abbot)

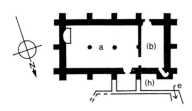

Croxden Abbey (abbot)

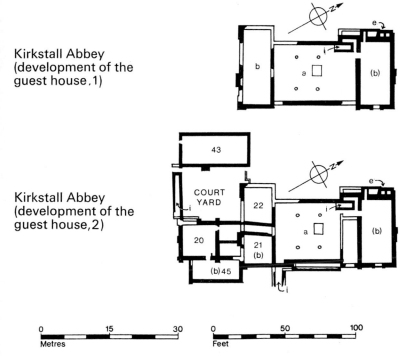

Kirkstall Abbey
(development of the
guest house,1)

Kirkstall Abbey
(development of the
guest house,2)

0   15   30
Metres

0   50   100
Feet

Fig 24   Presidents' and guests' houses

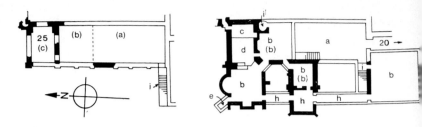

Castle Acre Priory (development of prior's house, first floor)

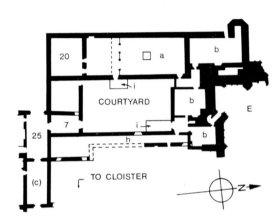

Westminster Abbey (abbot)

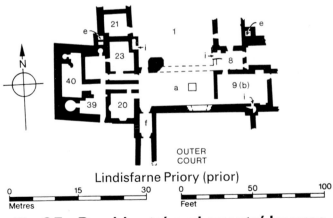

Lindisfarne Priory (prior)

OUTER
COURT

0	15	30
Metres		

0	50	100
Feet		

Fig 25 Presidents' and guests' houses

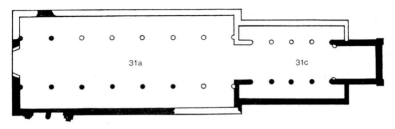

Canterbury Cathedral-monastery

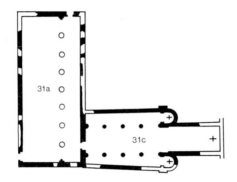

St Augustine's Abbey, Canterbury

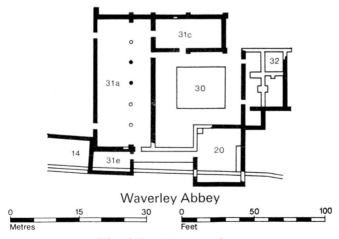

Waverley Abbey

Fig 26 Farmeries

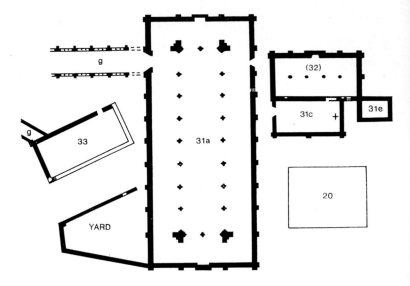

Fountains Abbey

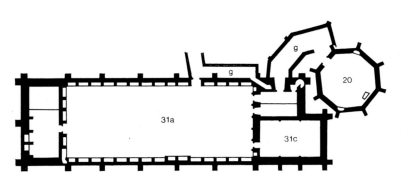

Furness Abbey

Metres

Feet

Fig 27 Farmeries

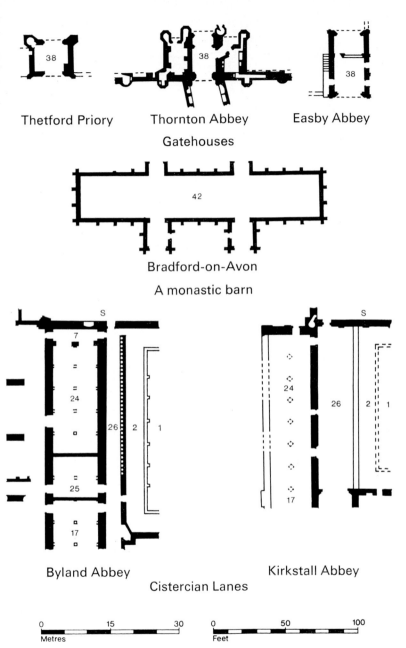

Thetford Priory   Thornton Abbey   Easby Abbey

Gatehouses

Bradford-on-Avon

A monastic barn

Byland Abbey   Kirkstall Abbey

Cistercian Lanes

Metres   Feet

Fig 28   Gatehouses, Cistercian lanes and a monastic barn

Caretaker occupation (twelfth century)

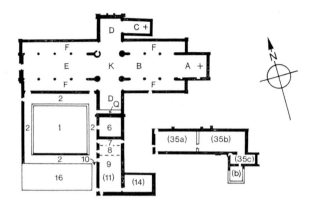

The fully developed priory (thirteenth century)

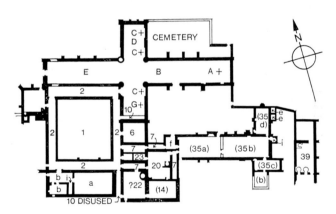

The reduced priory (fifteenth century)

Fig 29 Finchale Priory, development

Key to the plans

+	altar	14	reredorter
A	presbytery	15	lay brethren's reredorter
B	quire	16	frater
C	chapel	17	lay brethren's frater
D	transept	18	lavatory
E	nave	19	pulpit
F	aisle	20	kitchen
G	Lady Chapel	21	buttery
H	sacristy or vestry	22	pantry
I	ambulatory	23	larder
J	Galilee porch	24	cellar or store
K	tower	25	outer parlour
L	rood screen	26	lane
M	pulpitum	27	cell
N	shrine	28	garden
O	watching loft	29	conduit
P	tomb	30	little cloister
Q	night stairs	31	farmery
R	walking place	32	infirmarer's lodging
S	lay brethren's quire	33	misericord
T	eucharistic oven	34	lay brethren's farmery
U	lectern	35	president's lodging
V	font	36	guests' lodging
W	holy water	37	window house
X	sanctuary chamber	38	gatehouse
Y	organs	39	bakehouse
Z	clock	40	brewhouse
AA	bishop's throne	41	dairy
BB	processional markers	42	granary
CC	crypt	43	stables
		44	poultry
1	cloister garth	45	stores
2	cloister alley	46	wood store
3	carrells		
4	books	a	hall
5	vestibule	b	chamber
6	chapter house	c	chapel
7	passage	d	study
8	inner parlour	e	garderobe
9	warming house	f	porch
10	day stairs	g	pentice
11	dorter	h	gallery
12	lay brethren's dorter	i	stairs
13	lay sisters' dorter		

Letters and numbers in parentheses indicate rooms on the floor above

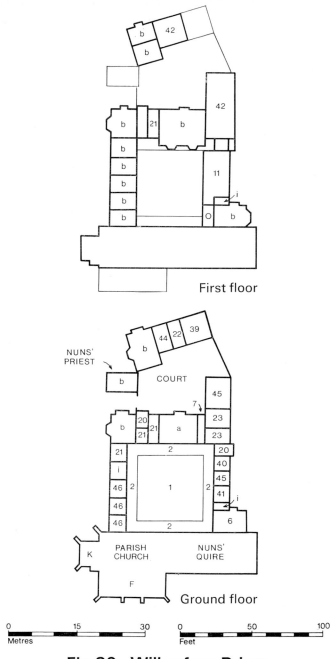

Fig 30   Wilberfoss Priory
A small Benedictine nunnery on the eve of the dissolution

Glossary

of words not explained in the text

Aisle	Part of a church on either side of the nave or chancel
Apse	A semi-circular end to or projection from a building
Apsidal	Ending in an apse
Arcade	A line of arches
Bay	A structural division of the length of a building or roof
Buttery	A room for storing and serving drink
Buttress	A projecting support to a wall
Chancel	The eastern part of a church
Chantry	An endowment for masses to be said for a special intention
Choir	Quire
Claustral	To do with or belonging to a cloister
Conduit	An artificial water supply
Corrodian	A layman for whom board and lodging in a religious house was purchased for a lump sum of money
Crossing	Central space where the east–west axis of a church is crossed by the north–south transepts
Garderobe	A latrine or privy
Lady Chapel	Chapel dedicated to "Our Lady, the Blessed Virgin"
Lectern	A reading desk
Liturgy	The Church's form of public worship
Martyrology	A list of martyrs
Nave	Part of a church extending westwards from the crossing
Newel stairs	Spiral stairs
Novice	A member of a religious community who is under probation
Obituary	A register of deaths
Pantry	A room for storing and serving bread and other provisions
Pentice	A penthouse or lean-to
Piscina	A small basin with a drain beside an altar, in which to cleanse the sacramental vessels
Presbytery	Eastern part of a church, reserved to the clergy and containing the principal altar
Quire	Part of a church between the nave and presbytery, appropriated to those singing the service
Religious	Belonging to a monastic Order
Reliquary	Receptacle for the relics of a saint

Reredos	An ornamental screen at the back of an altar
Screens passage	Passage at the lower or kitchen end of a hall
Sedilia	Seats in the presbytery for the officiating clergy
Stalls	Rows of carved wooden seats lining the walls of the quire
Tau cross	A cross in the shape of a letter T
Transept	Transverse part of a cruciform church, set at right angles to the main axis
Undercroft	A chamber, usually vaulted, serving to support principal chamber above
Vault	An arched stone or brick roof

Index

of English and Welsh Religious Houses mentioned in the Text

Religious houses marked with an asterisk are in the care of the Department of the Environment and are normally open to visitors daily at reasonable hours. Many others also are open to inspection, but appearance in this index is no guarantee of the fact in particular cases.

Other religious houses wholly or partly in the care of the Department of the Environment

General Index

Printed in England for Her Majesty's Stationery Office
by The Campfield Press, St. Albans

(20625)   Dd. 289916   K68   6/76

This series of illustrated Guides to Ancient Monuments maintained by the Department of the Environment is planned to cover England, Wales and Scotland.

Other volumes available:

New Series:
1 NORTHERN ENGLAND. 75p (84½p).
2 SOUTHERN ENGLAND. 60p (71p).
4 WALES. 75p (88p).
5 CYMRU (*in Welsh*)
6 CASTLES (ENGLAND AND WALES). 35p (44½p).

Old Series:
3 EAST ANGLIA AND THE MIDLANDS. 55p (64½p).
4 SOUTH WALES AND MONMOUTHSHIRE. 50p (58p).
5 NORTH WALES. 35p (43p).
6 SCOTLAND. 30p (39½p).
  SCOTTISH ABBEYS. 60p (73p).
  SCOTTISH CASTLES. 27½p (37p).

Prices in brackets include postage